Quick Breads

EVERYBODY'S FAVORITES FROM DINNER BREADS TO DESSERTS

BARRY BLUESTEIN
and
KEVIN MORRISSEY

CB
CONTEMPORARY
BOOKS
CHICAGO

Library of Congress Cataloging-in-Publication Data

Bluestein, Barry.
    Quick breads : everybody's favorites from dinner breads to
desserts / Barry Bluestein and Kevin Morrissey.
      p.   cm.
    Includes index.
    ISBN 0-8092-3973-6 (pbk.)
    1. Bread.   I. Morrissey, Kevin.   II. Title.
TX769.B625   1991
641.8'15—dc20   91-23669
                                            CIP

Published by Contemporary Books, Inc.
Two Prudential Plaza, Chicago, Illinois 60601-6790
Manufactured in the United States of America
International Standard Book Number: 0-8092-3973-6

Fondly dedicated to Elaine Barlas, Linda Gray, and Claudia Clark Potter, three disparate friends whose only common threads are their fervent devotion to their individual eccentricities and their bemused delight in ours

CONTENTS

Acknowledgments ix

1 Introduction... 1
   Quick Tips on Ingredients 2
   Quick Tips on Equipment and Technique 3

2 All-Time Favorites: The Traditions and Traditions Updated
   Farmhouse Cornbread 6
   Pueblo Cornbread with Jalapeño Peppers 8
   Sara Bluestein's Date Nut Bread 10
   Toasted Coconut Date Bread 12
   Grandma's Chocolate Bread 14
   Banana Peanut Chocolate Bread 15
   Traditional Banana Bread 16
   Golden Banana Nut Bread 17
   Blueberry Sour Cream Streusel 18
   Blueberry Wild Rice Bread................................ 19
   Victorian Gingerbread 20
   Orange Gingerbread 21

Old-Fashioned Beer Bread 22
Stout Bread à la Lucy 23

3 Savory Breads
Olive Almond Bread 26
Swiss Cheese Olive Bread 28
Chi-Town Sausage and Cheese Loaf 30
Caraway Tea Bread 32
Honey Bear Bran Bread 33
Savory Scallion Curry Bread 34
Salmon Cream Cheese Bread 36
Betty Morrissey's Irish Soda Bread 38
Banned-in-Boston Brown Bread 40
Peanut Butter Bread 41
1890s Raisin Spice Bread 42
Brandied Sweet Potato Bread 44
Popover Bread 45
Classic Spoonbread 46
Fresh Herb Bread 47
Spinach Feta Cheese Loaf 48
Cheddar Dill Bread 50
Dixie Cornbread with Bacon 51
Cheddar Cheese Cornbread 52
Dark Zucchini Bread 53
Port Wine and Fig Bread 54
Croque Monsieur Loaf 55

4 Sweet Breads
Applesauce Nut Bread 58
Bobbi's Raisin Rum Tea Bread 60
Rhubarb Bread 62
Maple Walnut Fig Bread 63
Mandarin Orange Nut Bread 64
Strawberry Cheese Loaf 66
Strawberry Walnut Bread 68

Lemon Poppy Seed Tea Bread 69
Raspberry Cinnamon Swirl 70
Marcia Jo's Pear Brandy and Honey Bread 72
Pear Mango Bread 74
Papaya Filbert Bread 75
Cranberry Apricot Loaf 76
Pumpkin Pie Bread 77
Door County Sour Cherry Bread 78
Orange Marmalade Bread 80
Butterscotch–Butterscotch Chip Bread .81
Bubba's Poppy Seed Bread 82
Jill's Oatmeal Raisin Bread 84
Orange Pecan Tea Bread 85
Raspberry Macadamia Nut Delight 86
Nutty Maple Yogurt Bread 87
Apricot Cream Cheese Swirl 88
Cinnamon Raisin Bread 90
Nutty Prune Bread 91
Pineapple Zucchini Bread 92
Linda's Chocolate Chip Cheesecake Bread 93
Claudia's Apple Cinnamon Swirl 94
Lemon Rice Bread 96

5 "I Can't Believe It's a Quick Bread!"
Quick Old-Fashioned Pumpernickel 98
Braided Egg Bread 99
New York Caraway Onion Rye 100
Rosemary Garlic Bread 102
Patty's Pepper Cheese Bread 104
Pesto Bread 106
Chocolate Chip Babka 108
Cream Cheese Pineapple Loaf 110

Index 113

ACKNOWLEDGMENTS

Special thanks to Jill Van Cleave for her advice, support, and just for being Jill—an always warm and friendly face at the door, often, unbeknownst to her, when we most need it.

Thanks also to Barbara Grunes, Rob Humrickhouse, Tim Kivel, Patty Oria, and Lucy Saunders for their seemingly endless favors and for their ongoing support for us and for Season To Taste Books.

1
INTRODUCTION

Very few of life's so-called little pleasures are as simple, as satisfying, and as pervasive as baking bread. The inherent sense of fulfillment and well-being that derive from combining ingredients to produce this most basic of foods has survived through the ages, providing at least as much nourishment for the soul as for the body. And the aroma of freshly baked bread wafting through a home instantly pushes all sorts of subliminal comfort buttons, as even the most novice real estate agent will advise.

In the past, baking skills were passed down from generation to generation almost as assiduously as reading and writing skills. Our grandparents would have thought of a home where no baking took place as somehow sad and barren. During more recent decades, however, "store-bought" became the norm, and the aroma of fresh-baked bread began to disappear from our kitchens.

Happily, many Americans are now rediscovering the joys of hearth and home, including those of the kitchen. But the mystique of baking can easily seem overwhelming to a generation nurtured on takeout, and many traditional bread recipes require a time commitment not in keeping with today's harried schedules.

Our premise in writing *Quick Breads* is that the rewards of bread baking far outweigh the perceived obstacles that keep many a would-be baker hovering nervously at the kitchen door. We developed our recipes with a focus on the time constraints of modern life and with an eye toward demystifying the science of baking without dispelling the magic of the art. We think you'll be amazed at what you can produce quickly and without the use of yeast (see especially the chapter "I Can't Believe It's a Quick Bread!").

Our goal is to enable you to have your home smelling like a bakery within an hour and to produce tasty, attractive breads for any occasion, using readily available ingredients and with no need for a lot of specialized equipment. All of the techniques you'll need are detailed in this book.

All of these breads bake in less than an hour, and most of the recipes can be executed from start to finish in not much more than that, give or take a few anticipatory moments for your creation to cool before serving. None require the dreaded yeast that often leaves novice bakers rereading *War and Peace* while waiting for the dough to rise. Only one recipe calls for kneading the dough, and that for only about 30 seconds instead of the long and laborious process usually required for bread.

All of the ingredients called for in these recipes are readily available in almost any supermarket. In short, if you leave the office in time for a quick shop on the way home, your quick bread can be ready to serve by the end of the evening news.

QUICK TIPS ON INGREDIENTS

Bananas: A few recipes call for the use of very ripe bananas (which have darkened and become soft). To expedite the ripening of bananas, pop them into the oven at its lowest setting for about 25 minutes, remove, and allow to cool before using.

Butter: Butter is much more easily creamed when softened to room temperature first. When melted butter is called for, melt on top of the stove in a small skillet or in a microwave oven at full power for about 1 minute.

Eggs: Many recipes call for the addition of well-beaten eggs. Trust us and be sure to beat the eggs first, even when they subsequently are to be beaten into other ingredients. In some recipes, we suggest the use of an electric mixer (see *Quick Tips on Equipment and Technique*) and then call for adding eggs. If you are going to give the electric mixer a rest and proceed to mix by hand, always beat the eggs before combining with other ingredients.

Flours and Grains: Don't be intimidated by a recipe that calls for the inclusion of a flour or grain with which you're not familiar. Your local grocery store probably carries a wide selection these days.

Fruit: When fruit is called for, use canned (drained thoroughly) if fresh is not readily available. Frozen fruit can yield excess water that will give your bread a most unappealing spongelike texture.

Nuts: When chopped nuts are called for, keep a light touch if you are going to use a food processor. A few seconds too long and your chopped nuts will be dust that adds no crunch to the bread.

Ingredient Temperatures: It's best to let all refrigerated ingredients reach room temperature before use. When it makes a significant difference to the recipe, we specifically call for allowing ingredients to come to room temperature. But this is not a bad idea to follow all the time, as combining ice-cold ingredients and flour can inhibit the rising of the dough.

QUICK TIPS ON EQUIPMENT AND TECHNIQUE

Mixers and Mixing: In many recipes, we suggest the use of an electric mixer just to save time and effort. In the case of almost all procedures but beating egg whites, however, you can do just fine beating by hand with a wire whisk if you have the stamina. Whenever the use of an electric mixer is suggested, know that you can proceed safely through that step of the recipe without the aid of technology. We'll take you on to another step and clearly say so if you then need to switch to incorporating ingredients by hand.

Combining Ingredients: Recipes are divided into steps that initially separate the preparation of components subsequently to be combined. All recipes ultimately call for the combination of a dry flour mixture with wet ingredients. Once the flour mixture is added, it's important not to overly beat the batter in order to avoid having a bread with a tough texture. We recommend blending, with a wooden spoon, only until the dry ingredients are absorbed into the batter. If you are using one of those large, heavy-duty stationary mixers (as opposed to using the hand-held variety or mixing manually), use the paddle attachment rather than blending ingredients with the beaters.

Loaf Pans: Most of our recipes are baked in loaf pans. In testing, we used the common 9¼-inch variety. If you vary the size, just remember to fill pans up about ⅔ of the way to allow ideal room for rising. Especially if batter is thick, be sure to push down into the corners of the pan to ensure an evenly shaped loaf.

Unless we specifically call for greasing the pan with a particular substance, the choice is yours. We prefer using butter, 1 to 2 tablespoons of which will serve to grease the standard 9¼-inch loaf pan. But feel free to use vegetable oil, shortening, or a spray-on substance (ignore any directions to flour pan if using a spray). If you have parchment liners, they may be used in lieu of greasing.

Many recipes call for pans to be dusted with flour (which makes life a whole lot easier when it's time to remove the bread from the pan). Put 1 to 2 tablespoons of flour as needed into the greased pan and swirl until pan is lightly coated, dumping any excess flour that remains.

When baking pans are called for, remember that glass pans conduct heat faster than metal pans. Check the bread a little sooner if you use glass.

Miniloaf and Muffin Pans: Although our recipes are geared toward the use of large loaf pans, you can easily adapt them for miniloaves (which produce the perfect size dinner loaf for two) or for muffins. In general, the batter for 1 large (about 9¼-inch) loaf pan will fill 3 miniloaf pans (about 5¾ inches long, and proportionately narrower and shallower). Reduce baking time for miniloaves by about 10 minutes. The same amount of batter will make a dozen muffins, which should be baked 10 to 15 minutes less than a large loaf. (When using muffin tins, remember to grease not only the wells but also the top surface between the wells.)

Baking Times: We reinforce the eternal cookbook caveat. Baking times are approximate and based on our testing in our oven, and all ovens are different. To be safe, start checking the bread at least 5 minutes before the low end of the estimated baking time. "Doneness" can be measured in several ways—when a tester comes out clean, when the center of the dough is firm to the touch, or when the dough begins to separate from the edges of the pan.

Cooling: After removing bread from the oven, let it sit for a few minutes. Then remove it from the pan and transfer the bread to a cooling rack until you're ready to serve it.

Storing: By all means, you can freeze baked breads (in sealable plastic bags) for later enjoyment. Just thaw to room temperature before serving, or thaw, wrap in damp paper toweling, and microwave at full power for 2 to 3 minutes until moist and piping hot!

2
ALL-TIME FAVORITES:
THE TRADITIONS AND
TRADITIONS UPDATED

◆

FARMHOUSE CORNBREAD

We like to prepare this hearty cornbread in the traditional country way—baking it in a preheated cast-iron skillet, which produces a crusty, dark brown bottom. A baking pan of similar size will work in a pinch, but the crust will not be as distinguished. If you're using a baking pan, grease the pan well, but do not preheat.

1½ cups yellow cornmeal
½ cup all-purpose flour
1 teaspoon baking powder
1 teaspoon baking soda
1 teaspoon salt
2 large eggs, separated
1¾ cups buttermilk
⅓ cup (5⅓ tablespoons) unsalted
    butter, melted, plus 2
    tablespoons to grease
    skillet.

1. Place a heavy-bottomed 10-inch skillet (preferably cast iron) with an ovenproof handle in oven and preheat to 450°F.

2. Sift cornmeal, flour, baking powder, baking soda, and salt together into a large mixing bowl.

3. In a separate bowl, beat egg yolks well. Whisk buttermilk thoroughly into beaten yolks. Whisk in melted butter.

4. Using an electric mixer, beat egg whites until stiff (but not dry) peaks are formed. Set aside.

5. Add buttermilk/egg mixture to the cornmeal/flour mixture and blend well with a wooden spoon until free of lumps. Using a slotted spoon, gently fold in beaten egg whites.

6. Remove heated skillet from oven. Put remaining butter in skillet and carefully swirl until butter has melted and coated entire surface. Pour cornmeal mixture into skillet and return to oven. Bake 16 to 18 minutes, until edges of cornbread are deep brown and center is golden. Serve hot with plenty of butter.

Makes 1 loaf

PUEBLO CORNBREAD WITH JALAPEÑO PEPPERS

Guaranteed to send aficionados of the hot and spicy into ecstasy! We like to serve this southwestern-style cornbread with black beans and salsa, but it will perk up a wide range of entrées equally well. Wear rubber gloves when preparing the jalapeño peppers, and be sure to remove all seeds and rinse the peppers under cold running water before chopping.

1⅓ cups yellow cornmeal
⅔ cup all-purpose flour
1 tablespoon baking powder
1 teaspoon salt
⅛ teaspoon cayenne pepper
1 teaspoon ground cumin
1 cup sour cream
⅓ cup half and half
1 large egg, well beaten
¼ cup (4 tablespoons) unsalted
    butter, melted
¼ cup seeded and finely diced
    jalapeño peppers
1 small can (about 7 ounces)
    corn kernels, drained
½ cup diced scallion (4–6
    scallions, white and light
    green parts only)

1. Preheat oven to 425°F.

2. Sift cornmeal, flour, baking powder, salt, cayenne pepper, and cumin together into a bowl.

3. In a large mixing bowl, whisk sour cream and half and half together well. Add beaten egg and whisk in thoroughly. Whisk in melted butter. Add cornmeal/flour mixture and blend well with a wooden spoon. Stir in jalapeño peppers, corn kernels, and scallion.

4. Pour mixture into a well-greased 11″ × 8½″ baking pan. Bake 20 to 25 minutes, until edges begin to brown. Serve hot.

Makes 1 loaf

SARA BLUESTEIN'S DATE NUT BREAD

Barry's mom provided this recipe for a dense, old-fashioned date nut round. The trick to making perfect rounds is simply to bake in aluminum cans. The rounds can be frozen right in the cans and steamed back to perfection whenever the urge strikes.

1 cup chopped dried pitted
   dates
2 teaspoons baking soda
1½ cups boiling water
2 large eggs, separated
2 tablespoons unsalted butter,
   melted
1¼ cups sugar
⅓ cup grated orange (grate the
   whole orange, unpeeled,
   and use peel, pulp, and
   juice)
3½ cups all-purpose flour,
   divided into 2-cup and
   1½-cup measures
1 cup chopped walnuts
2 teaspoons vanilla extract

1. Preheat oven to 350°F.

2. Mix dates and baking soda in a small bowl. Add water and stir well. Set aside and allow mixture to cool to room temperature.

3. Grease and lightly flour the insides of 6 tall medium-sized (about 14- to 16-ounce) aluminum cans that have been emptied and thoroughly cleaned.

4. Slightly beat egg yolks in a large mixing bowl. Add melted butter, sugar, and grated orange. Mix thoroughly. Stir in 2 cups of the flour. Stir in date mixture, walnuts, and vanilla. Add remaining 1½ cups flour and blend well.

5. Using an electric mixer, beat egg whites until stiff (but not dry) peaks are formed. Using a slotted spoon, gently fold into mixture.

6. Pour mixture evenly into prepared cans, filling cans only half full. Bake 30 to 40 minutes, until a tester inserted into the center comes out clean.

Makes 6 rounds

TOASTED COCONUT DATE BREAD

This is definitely not the date nut bread your mother used to make. It has a distinctive toasted nut flavor not at all like the usual sweet coconut taste. The extra work of shredding fresh coconut is well worth the effort. Besides, when was the last time you followed a recipe that told you to whack something with a hammer?

1 medium-sized coconut
2 cups all-purpose flour
1 teaspoon baking powder
2 teaspoons baking soda
½ teaspoon salt
2 large eggs, well beaten
½ cup sugar
⅓ cup (5⅓ tablespoons) unsalted
    butter, melted
½ cup coarsely chopped dried
    pitted dates

1. Using a hammer and a nail, puncture the "eyes" (the dark, circular indentations on top) of the coconut. Drain the milk (the clear liquid of the coconut) into a measuring cup. (You will need ¾ cup coconut milk for this recipe. If the coconut does not yield enough milk, add enough whole milk to bring the total volume to ¾ cup.) Set aside. Wrap the drained coconut in a towel and whack the long side with the hammer until the shell cracks apart. Discard the fragments of shell, scrape off the brown inner skin, and shred the white coconut meat to yield 1⅓ cups.

2. Preheat oven to 375°F.

3. Sift flour, baking powder, baking soda, and salt together into a bowl.

4. Put beaten eggs and sugar into a large mixing bowl. Beat with an electric mixer. While continuing to beat, add melted butter, then coconut milk.

5. Stir in shredded coconut and dates. Add flour mixture and blend well with a wooden spoon.

6. Pour mixture into a greased 9¼-inch loaf pan. Bake 35 to 45 minutes, until loaf begins to separate from the edges of the pan and a tester inserted into the center comes out clean.

Makes 1 loaf

GRANDMA'S CHOCOLATE BREAD

Dedicated with love to the many folks out there who don't think any meal is complete without a ration of chocolate. We didn't think any bread book would be complete without a recipe for old-time chocolate bread, just like Grandma used to make.

2 cups all-purpose flour
½ tablespoon baking powder
¼ teaspoon salt
3 1-ounce squares unsweetened
    baking chocolate
¼ cup (4 tablespoons) unsalted
    butter

½ cup sugar
1 cup buttermilk
1 large egg, well beaten
1 tablespoon unsweetened cocoa
    powder to dust pan

1. Preheat oven to 350°F.

2. Sift flour, baking powder, and salt together into a bowl.

3. Put chocolate and butter into the top part of a double boiler over boiling water. Cook over medium-low heat, stirring constantly, until melted and blended. (Chocolate and butter may also be melted in a microwave oven. Microwave about 1 minute at full power, then stir until chocolate has completely dissolved.) Remove from heat and stir sugar into mixture.

4. In a large mixing bowl, whisk buttermilk into beaten egg to a lemon hue. Beat in chocolate mixture. Add the flour mixture and blend well with a wooden spoon.

5. Pour into a well-greased 9¼-inch loaf pan that has been dusted (bottom and sides) with cocoa powder. Bake 45 to 55 minutes, until loaf begins to separate from the edges of the pan and a tester inserted into the center comes out clean.

Makes 1 loaf

BANANA PEANUT CHOCOLATE BREAD

Here, a hint of banana and the crunch of peanuts add new life to the traditional chocolate bread. It's wonderful topped with ice cream or whipped cream—rather like a reincarnated banana split.

1½ cups all-purpose flour
½ teaspoon baking powder
¼ teaspoon baking soda
½ teaspoon salt
½ cup unsweetened cocoa
    powder, plus 1 tablespoon
    to dust pan
½ cup pure clover honey
2 tablespoons sugar
6 tablespoons unsalted butter,
    softened to room
    temperature

¾ teaspoon vanilla extract
1 large egg
¾ cup mashed very ripe banana
    (about 2 medium-sized
    bananas)
2 tablespoons sour cream
⅓ cup coarsely chopped, roasted
    unsalted peanuts

1. Preheat oven to 350°F.

2. Sift flour, baking powder, baking soda, salt, and cocoa powder together into a large mixing bowl.

3. Using an electric mixer, cream honey and sugar with butter (beat until sugar is dissolved and mixture is creamy). Beat in vanilla, egg, banana, and sour cream, mixing well after each addition.

4. Add to the flour mixture and blend with a wooden spoon just until flour is absorbed. Stir in nuts.

5. Pour mixture into a greased 9¼-inch loaf pan that has been dusted (bottom and sides) with cocoa powder. Bake 40 to 50 minutes, until loaf begins to separate from the edges of the pan and a tester inserted into the center comes out clean.

Makes 1 loaf

TRADITIONAL BANANA BREAD

Close your eyes, inhale deeply, take a bite—and you'll almost certainly be transported back to Mom's kitchen.

1½ cups all-purpose flour
2 teaspoons baking powder
½ teaspoon salt
½ cup sugar
2 large eggs
½ cup buttermilk
1 teaspoon vanilla extract
1½ teaspoons ground cinnamon
¼ teaspoon ground nutmeg
¼ cup dark brown sugar, firmly
    packed
½ cup raw "quick" oats
1¼ cups mashed very ripe
    banana (about 3
    medium-sized bananas)

1. Preheat oven to 375°F.

2. Sift flour, baking powder, salt, and sugar together into a bowl.

3. In a large mixing bowl, beat eggs well with an electric mixer. Beat in buttermilk. Add vanilla extract, cinnamon, and nutmeg, mixing well. Beat in brown sugar.

4. Stir in oats. Add banana and mix well. Add flour mixture and blend well with a wooden spoon.

5. Pour mixture into a greased and floured (bottom and sides dusted with flour) 9¼-inch loaf pan. Bake 50 to 55 minutes, until loaf begins to separate from the edges of the pan and a tester inserted into the center comes out clean.

Makes 1 loaf

GOLDEN BANANA NUT BREAD

This version of this perennial favorite is lighter, both in texture and in color, than the traditional variety. It actually looks like banana, since there's no brown sugar to darken the loaf.

2 cups all-purpose flour
½ tablespoon baking powder
½ teaspoon salt
¼ cup (4 tablespoons) unsalted
    butter, softened to room
    temperature
⅔ cup sugar
2 large eggs
1 cup mashed very ripe banana
    (2–3 medium-sized
    bananas)
⅓ cup buttermilk
½ cup chopped walnuts

1. Preheat oven to 375°F.

2. Sift flour, baking powder, and salt together into a bowl.

3. In a large mixing bowl, cream butter and sugar with an electric mixer (beat until sugar is dissolved and mixture is creamy). While continuing to beat, add eggs one at a time.

4. Stir in banana, buttermilk, and walnuts. Add one-half of the flour mixture and blend thoroughly with a wooden spoon. Repeat with remaining half of flour mixture.

5. Pour mixture into a greased and floured (bottom and sides dusted with flour) 9¼-inch loaf pan. Bake 40 to 50 minutes, until loaf begins to separate from the edges of the pan and a tester inserted into the center comes out clean.

Makes 1 loaf

BLUEBERRY SOUR CREAM STREUSEL

Many consider this bread the ultimate comfort food. Just settle into a familiar chair armed with a good cup of coffee, the Sunday paper, and a generous slice of this bread.

BREAD
1½ cups all-purpose flour
2 teaspoons baking powder
1 teaspoon baking soda
¼ teaspoon salt
½ cup sugar
2 large eggs
1 cup sour cream
1 cup small wild blueberries
    (fresh or canned; drained if
    canned)

TOPPING
1 tablespoon all-purpose flour
2 tablespoons sugar
1 tablespoon unsalted butter,
    softened to room
    temperature

1. Preheat oven to 375°F.

2. Sift flour, baking powder, baking soda, salt, and sugar together into a bowl.

3. In a large mixing bowl, thoroughly beat eggs. Add sour cream and beat well. Stir in blueberries. Add flour mixture and blend with a wooden spoon just until flour is absorbed into liquid ingredients.

4. Pour mixture into a greased and floured (bottom and sides dusted with flour) 9¼-inch loaf pan.

5. To make topping, combine flour, sugar, and butter in a small bowl. Beat to the consistency of scrambled eggs with a fork. Sprinkle evenly over the top of the loaf. Bake 40 to 45 minutes, until loaf begins to separate from the edges of the pan and a tester inserted into the center comes out clean.

Makes 1 loaf

BLUEBERRY WILD RICE BREAD

Wild rice adds just the right savory twist to this updated classic. Be sure not to overcook the rice—you want it to be a bit crunchy when added to this recipe so that its full-bodied flavor and texture can be appreciated.

1⅓ cups all-purpose flour
2 teaspoons baking powder
¾ teaspoon baking soda
½ teaspoon salt
¼ cup sugar
¾ cup milk
1 large egg, well beaten
½ teaspoon ground cardamom

1⅓ cups cooked wild rice,
    cooled to room temperature
1 cup small wild blueberries
    (fresh or canned; drained if
    canned), coated with 1
    tablespoon all-purpose
    flour

1. Preheat oven to 350°F.

2. Sift flour, baking powder, baking soda, salt, and sugar together into a bowl.

3. Combine milk and beaten egg in a large mixing bowl. Whisk together well. Mix in cardamom. Add rice and whisk thoroughly.

4. Add flour mixture and blend well with a wooden spoon. Gently fold in blueberries, taking care not to crush them.

5. Pour mixture into a greased and floured (bottom and sides dusted with flour) 9¼-inch loaf pan. Bake 45 to 55 minutes, until loaf begins to separate from the edges of the pan and a tester inserted into the center comes out clean.

Makes 1 loaf

VICTORIAN GINGERBREAD

Countless variations of gingerbread have been popular since before the turn of the century, and for good reason, since few things conjure up hearth and home as much as the aroma of warm gingerbread. This is a light and refreshing version, redolent of Victorian kitchens.

⅔ cup (10⅔ tablespoons)
    unsalted butter
2 cups dark unsulphured
    molasses
1 tablespoon baking soda
1 tablespoon ground cinnamon
1 tablespoon ground ginger
1 teaspoon ground nutmeg
1 large egg
1 cup buttermilk
3 cups all-purpose flour

1. Preheat oven to 375°F.

2. Combine butter and molasses in a heavy saucepan and bring to a boil over medium heat. Stir in baking soda, cinnamon, ginger, and nutmeg. Remove from heat.

3. In a large mixing bowl, thoroughly beat egg with an electric mixer. Beat in buttermilk. While continuing to beat, add butter/molasses mixture.

4. Sift flour directly into mixture and blend well with a wooden spoon.

5. Pour mixture into a greased 11″ × 8½″ baking pan. Bake 20 to 30 minutes, until loaf begins to separate from the edges of the pan and a tester inserted into the center comes out clean.

Makes 1 loaf

ORANGE GINGERBREAD

This is a dense, dark gingerbread—slightly oriental in character due to the pairing of orange and ginger—sure to tantalize modern taste buds.

½ cup (8 tablespoons) unsalted butter, softened to room temperature
½ cup sugar
¾ cup dark unsulphured molasses
1 teaspoon baking soda
1 teaspoon ground ginger

2 teaspoons ground cinnamon
¼ teaspoon ground nutmeg
2 large eggs
½ cup orange juice (preferably freshly squeezed)
½ tablespoon grated orange rind
2 cups all-purpose flour

1. Preheat oven to 375°F.

2. Using an electric mixer, cream butter and sugar (beat until sugar is dissolved and mixture is creamy).

3. Combine with molasses in a saucepan. Bring to a boil over medium heat, stirring constantly. Stir in baking soda, ginger, cinnamon, and nutmeg. Remove from heat.

4. In a large mixing bowl, whisk eggs until well beaten. Whisk in molasses/butter mixture thoroughly. Add orange juice and beat well. Add orange rind. Whisk in flour.

5. Pour mixture into a greased and floured (bottom and sides dusted with flour) 9¼-inch loaf pan. Bake 25 to 35 minutes, until loaf begins to separate from the edges of the pan and a tester inserted into the center comes out clean.

Makes 1 loaf

OLD-FASHIONED BEER BREAD

This bread provides the perfect base for those Monday night football game Dagwood sandwiches. Grab a brat, grab a brew, and don't hold the mustard!

2 cups oat flour blend (a
    prepackaged blend of wheat
    and oat flours)
⅔ cup whole-wheat flour
⅓ cup wheat bran
1 teaspoon baking powder
¼ teaspoon salt
⅓ cup sugar
3 tablespoons unsalted butter,
    melted
12 ounces beer

1. Preheat oven to 350°F.

2. In a large bowl, mix together flours, bran, baking powder, salt, and sugar.

3. Make a well in the center of the dry ingredients. Pour in melted butter and beer. Stir with a wooden spoon just until blended.

4. Pour mixture into greased 9¼-inch loaf pan. Bake 45 to 55 minutes, until loaf begins to separate from the edges of the pan and a tester inserted into the center comes out clean.

Makes 1 loaf

STOUT BREAD A LA LUCY

We dedicate this recipe to our friend Lucy, a food journalist and one of the nation's foremost experts on cuisine à la beer. This robust bread derives its personality from the roasted malt of the dark Irish or English ale.

2 cups all-purpose flour
1 cup medium rye flour
½ teaspoon baking soda
½ teaspoon salt
½ teaspoon caraway seeds
¼ cup dark brown sugar, firmly
    packed
¼ cup (4 tablespoons) unsalted
    butter, melted
12 ounces stout (heavy-bodied
    dark ale)

1. Preheat oven to 350°F.

2. In a large mixing bowl, mix together flours, baking soda, salt, and caraway seeds.

3. In a separate bowl, whisk together brown sugar and melted butter until sugar is dissolved.

4. Make a well in the center of the flour mixture. Pour in brown sugar/butter mixture and stout. Stir with a wooden spoon just until blended.

5. Pour mixture into greased 9¼-inch loaf pan. Bake 45 to 55 minutes, until loaf begins to separate from the edges of the pan and a tester inserted into the center comes out clean.

Makes 1 loaf

3
SAVORY BREADS

◆

OLIVE ALMOND BREAD

Very rich and somewhat salty, this bread makes a terrific hors d'oeuvre, or it can serve as a light meal all by itself. While Kevin has been known to gobble up large quantities right out of the pan, we think that most people will find that a little goes a long way.

1 cup finely ground (to a
    powdery consistency)
    blanched almonds
2 cups all-purpose flour
2 teaspoons baking powder
⅛ teaspoon salt
⅔ cup sour cream
⅔ cup milk
2 tablespoons unsalted butter,
    melted
2 large eggs, well beaten
1 teaspoon crushed garlic
½ cup finely diced scallion
    (4–6 scallions, white and
    light green parts only)
½ tablespoon crumbled dried
    rosemary leaves
⅔ cup chopped calamata or
    Greek olives (rinse off
    brine and drain before
    chopping)
½ cup freshly grated Parmesan
    cheese
½ cup freshly grated Romano
    cheese

1. Preheat oven to 375°F.

2. Put almonds into a large mixing bowl. Sift flour, baking powder, and salt together into almonds and mix well.

3. In a separate bowl, whisk sour cream and milk together well. Add melted butter and beaten eggs. Continue to whisk until thoroughly blended. Add garlic, scallion, and rosemary. Mix well. Stir in olives.

4. Mix cheeses into flour mixture. Add liquid mixture and blend with a wooden spoon just until all ingredients are incorporated.

5. Pour mixture into a greased $9\frac{1}{4}$-inch loaf pan. Bake 40 to 50 minutes, until loaf begins to separate from the edges of the pan and a tester inserted into the center comes out clean.

Makes 1 loaf

SWISS CHEESE OLIVE BREAD

We love to serve this at cocktail parties, sliced thin and accompanied by a pitcher of very dry martinis. It also works well as bread for ham or pastrami sandwiches.

2 cups all-purpose flour
2 teaspoons baking powder
¼ teaspoon salt
2 large egg yolks
½ cup (8 tablespoons) unsalted
    butter, softened to room
    temperature
½ cup sugar
1 cup buttermilk
⅔ cup grated Swiss cheese
⅔ cup sliced pimiento-stuffed
    green olives
½ cup chopped walnuts
2 large egg whites

1. Preheat oven to 375°F.

2. Sift flour, baking powder, and salt together into a bowl.

3. Lightly beat egg yolks with a fork.

4. In a large mixing bowl, cream butter and sugar with an electric mixer (beat until sugar is dissolved and mixture is creamy). Beat in buttermilk, then beaten egg yolks.

5. Stir in Swiss cheese, olives, and walnuts.

6. In a separate bowl, beat egg whites with an electric mixer until stiff (but not dry) peaks are formed.

7. Add flour mixture to wet ingredients in large mixing bowl and blend with a wooden spoon. Using a slotted spoon, gently fold in beaten egg whites.

8. Pour into a greased and floured (bottom and sides dusted with flour) 9¼-inch loaf pan. Bake 45 to 55 minutes, until loaf begins to separate from the edges of the pan and a tester inserted into the center comes out clean.

Makes 1 loaf

CHI-TOWN SAUSAGE AND CHEESE LOAF

Designed to counter those chilly Lake Michigan breezes, this substantial Windy City treat is the perfect cold weather appetizer or snack.

BREAD
1¼ cups bulk pork sausage
    (preferably "country-style,"
    which is highly seasoned)
2 teaspoons ground thyme
1 large egg
⅔ cup milk
¼ cup (4 tablespoons) unsalted
    butter, melted
2¼ cups all-purpose flour
1 tablespoon baking powder
½ teaspoon salt
½ teaspoon sugar
2 tablespoons Dijon mustard
1 cup shredded extra-sharp
    cheddar cheese

TOPPING
1 beaten egg to paint dough
1 tablespoon dried onion flakes

1. Preheat oven to 350°F.

2. Combine sausage and thyme in a skillet. Cook over medium heat, breaking up meat with a wooden spoon, until crumbly but not browned. Using a slotted spoon, carefully transfer sausage onto paper toweling to drain.

3. In a large mixing bowl, beat egg. Whisk in milk, then melted butter. Sift flour, baking powder, salt, and sugar together directly into the mixture. Mix with a wooden spoon until a ball of dough is formed.

4. Transfer dough to a 1½- to 2-foot-long sheet of wax paper. Lay a second sheet of wax paper on top of the dough. Using a rolling pin, flatten and shape dough to an oblong about ½ inch thick. Remove the top sheet.

5. Coat the flattened dough with mustard. Cover with a layer of sausage, leaving a ½-inch border. Top with a layer of cheese.

6. Raise the left-hand side of the wax paper and fold dough about two-thirds of the way over onto itself, taking care not to force the filling out. Fold the right-hand side over, then crimp the ends to completely enclose filling. (The entire process is rather like folding a burrito.)

7. Carefully turn dough over and place seam side down, tucking ends under, on a greased cookie sheet that has been dusted with flour. Paint exposed surface of dough with beaten egg, using a pastry brush. With a sharp knife, make 2 slight diagonal incisions on top of dough (each about a third of the way along loaf). Sprinkle dried onion flakes on top. Bake 25 to 30 minutes, until a tester inserted into the side of the loaf comes out clean. Serve hot.

Makes 1 loaf

CARAWAY TEA BREAD

Its subtle, savory flavor and proper English accent make this bread an elegant addition to your tea table—but we won't tell if you eat it for breakfast, or even in the midst of a late-night refrigerator raid.

1 tablespoon caraway seeds
2 large eggs
¾ cup buttermilk
⅔ cup sugar
2 tablespoons unsalted butter,
    melted
½ teaspoon ground mace
2 cups all-purpose flour
2 teaspoons baking powder

1. Preheat oven to 375°F.

2. Put caraway seeds into a small bowl and crush with the back of a wooden spoon.

3. In a large mixing bowl, beat eggs well with an electric mixer. Beat in buttermilk, then sugar. While continuing to beat, add melted butter. Add mace and crushed caraway seeds. Beat well.

4. Sift flour and baking powder directly into mixture. Blend well with a wooden spoon.

5. Pour mixture into a greased and floured (bottom and sides dusted with flour) 9¼-inch loaf pan. Bake 45 to 55 minutes, until loaf begins to separate from the edges of the pan and a tester inserted into the center comes out clean.

Makes 1 loaf

HONEY BEAR BRAN BREAD

We think we've added just enough elements of honey cake to make this healthful bread really good, as well as good for you.

1¼ cups all-purpose flour
2½ teaspoons baking powder
¾ teaspoon baking soda
¼ teaspoon salt
½ teaspoon ground cloves
¾ cup pure clover honey
1 cup orange juice (preferably freshly squeezed)

1¼ cups oat bran
2 large eggs
¼ cup (4 tablespoons) unsalted butter, melted
¼ cup dark unsulphured molasses
⅔ cup dried currants

1. Preheat oven to 375°F.

2. Sift flour, baking powder, baking soda, salt, and cloves together into a bowl.

3. Whisk honey and orange juice together well. Add oat bran and mix thoroughly. Set aside.

4. In a large mixing bowl, whisk eggs until well beaten. Whisk in melted butter. Add molasses and mix in thoroughly. Whisk in oat bran mixture. Add flour mixture and blend well with a wooden spoon. Stir in currants.

5. Pour mixture into a greased and floured (bottom and sides dusted with flour) 9¼-inch loaf pan. Bake 45 to 55 minutes, until loaf begins to separate from the edges of the pan and a tester inserted into the center comes out clean.

Makes 1 loaf

SAVORY SCALLION CURRY BREAD

Forget frankincense, forget myrrh; we all know that curry is truly the incense of the gods. Its pervasive flavor, combined with the scallion, makes for a distinctive bread to grace your dinner table.

2½ cups all-purpose flour
2½ teaspoons baking powder
1 teaspoon baking soda
¼ teaspoon salt
1 tablespoon sugar
1 tablespoon unsalted butter for
    sautéing scallion, plus ¼
    cup (4 tablespoons), melted
⅓ cup chopped scallion
    (3–4 scallions, white and
    light green parts only)
1 tablespoon mild curry powder
½ teaspoon ground cumin
½ cup sour cream
½ cup milk
2 large eggs, well beaten
½ cup seedless golden raisins

1. Preheat oven to 375°F.

2. Sift flour, baking powder, baking soda, salt, and sugar together into a bowl.

3. Melt 1 tablespoon butter in a small skillet. Add scallion, curry powder, and cumin. Sauté over medium-low heat about 3 minutes, until scallion wilts.

4. In a large mixing bowl, whisk sour cream and milk well. Add beaten eggs and mix thoroughly. Whisk in melted butter. Stir in scallion mixture. Stir in raisins. Add flour mixture and blend well with a wooden spoon.

5. Pour mixture into a greased and floured (bottom and sides dusted with flour) 9¼-inch loaf pan. Bake 45 to 55 minutes, until loaf begins to separate from the edges of the pan and a tester inserted into the center comes out clean.

Makes 1 loaf

SALMON CREAM CHEESE BREAD

This is a bread that invariably finds its way to our Sunday brunch table. Who can resist the heavenly taste of smoked salmon and cream cheese, especially when it's so neatly packaged in a quick bread?

BREAD
1 large egg
⅔ cup milk
¼ cup (4 tablespoons) unsalted
    butter, melted
2 cups all-purpose flour
1 tablespoon baking powder
½ teaspoon salt
½ teaspoon sugar
1 tablespoon freshly ground
    pepper
1 3-ounce package cream cheese
4 slices smoked salmon
2 tablespoons chopped white
    onion

TOPPING
1 beaten egg to paint dough
1 tablespoon dried onion flakes

1. Preheat oven to 350°F.

2. In a large mixing bowl, beat egg. Whisk in milk, then melted butter. Sift flour, baking powder, salt, sugar, and pepper together directly into the mixture. Mix with a wooden spoon until a ball of dough is formed.

3. Transfer dough to a 1½- to 2-foot-long sheet of wax paper. Lay a second sheet of wax paper on top of the dough. Using a rolling pin, flatten and shape dough to form an oblong about ½ inch thick. Remove the top sheet of wax paper.

4. Spread cream cheese lengthwise over bottom third of the flattened dough, leaving a ¼-inch outer border. Cover with a layer of smoked salmon. Sprinkle chopped onion on top.

5. Raise the wax paper alongside the area where cheese has been spread and roll dough continuously over onto itself to form a log, then crimp the ends.

6. Place seam side down on a greased cookie sheet that has been dusted with flour, tucking ends under. Paint exposed surface of dough with beaten egg, using a pastry brush. With a sharp knife, make 2 slight diagonal incisions on top of dough (each about a third of the way along loaf). Sprinkle dried onion flakes on top. Bake 25 to 30 minutes, until a tester inserted into the side of the loaf comes out clean.

Makes 1 loaf

BETTY MORRISSEY'S IRISH SODA BREAD

Everybody loves breads—even Kevin's mother, who admits quite freely to making more reservations than recipes in recent years. Her recipe, which we've updated a bit to allow for the use of a food processor, produces a lighter-than-usual soda bread due to the addition of baking powder.

2 cups all-purpose flour
2 teaspoons baking powder
½ teaspoon baking soda
½ teaspoon salt
1 tablespoon sugar
3 tablespoons unsalted butter,
    softened to room
    temperature
¼ cup seedless raisins
¼ cup dried currants
1 teaspoon caraway seeds
1 cup buttermilk, plus 2
    tablespoons to paint dough

1. Preheat oven to 450°F.

2. Sift flour, baking powder, baking soda, salt, and sugar together into the bowl of a food processor. Add butter. Pulse 6–8 times quickly, until butter is cut into flour (flour is dotted with pea-size granules of butter).

3. Transfer mixture to a large bowl. Stir in raisins, currants, and caraway seeds. Add buttermilk. Mix with a wooden spoon until a ball of dough is formed.

4. Place dough into a greased 9-inch round baking pan. Press down lightly to spread dough, leaving about a 1-inch border around dough in bottom of pan. Paint exposed surface of dough with buttermilk, using a pastry brush. With a very sharp knife that has been dipped in flour, cut a shallow *X* across most of the top. Bake 5 minutes, then reduce heat to 325°F. Bake 30 to 40 minutes longer, until a tester inserted into the center comes out clean.

Makes 1 loaf

BANNED-IN-BOSTON BROWN BREAD

This is a hearty baked variation of the more traditional steamed brown bread of New England origin. But it tastes so good that we think the folks in Bean Town will forgive us.

1 cup all-purpose flour
2 cups whole-wheat flour
2 teaspoons baking soda
1 teaspoon salt
½ cup yellow cornmeal
¼ cup sugar
1 cup seedless raisins
2½ cups buttermilk
¼ cup dark unsulphured
    molasses
1 large egg, well beaten

1. Preheat oven to 350°F.

2. Sift flours, baking soda, and salt together into a large mixing bowl. Stir in cornmeal, sugar, and raisins.

3. In a separate bowl, whisk buttermilk and molasses together well. Whisk in beaten egg. Add to the flour mixture and blend with a wooden spoon.

4. Pour mixture into greased 9¼-inch loaf pan. Bake 50 to 55 minutes, until loaf begins to separate from the edges of the pan and a tester inserted into the center comes out clean.

Makes 1 loaf

PEANUT BUTTER BREAD

Peanut butter fans will love this very peanut-buttery bread. Just add the jam. The truly incorrigible peanut butter fanatic will probably want to top this with peanut butter as well.

2 cups all-purpose flour
1 teaspoon baking powder
¾ teaspoon baking soda
¼ teaspoon salt
2 tablespoons unsalted butter,
    melted
⅔ cup dark brown sugar, firmly
    packed
⅓ cup smooth peanut butter
1 large egg, well beaten
¼ cup roasted, unsalted peanuts
¼ cup seedless raisins
1 cup buttermilk

1. Preheat oven to 350°F.

2. Sift flour, baking powder, baking soda, and salt together into a bowl.

3. In a large mixing bowl, combine melted butter, brown sugar, and peanut butter. Beat well with an electric mixer. Add the beaten egg, beating until smooth. Add one-third of the flour mixture, continuing to beat until smooth.

4. Stir in peanuts, raisins, and buttermilk. Add remaining flour mixture and blend well with a wooden spoon.

5. Pour mixture into a greased and floured (bottom and sides dusted with flour) 9¼-inch loaf pan. Bake 45 to 55 minutes, until loaf begins to separate from the edges of the pan and a tester inserted into the center comes out clean.

Makes 1 loaf

1890s RAISIN SPICE BREAD

Raisin bread is usually sweet, sometimes overly so. But when you add the spices so favored in turn-of-the-century kitchens—ginger, cloves, and nutmeg—the bread takes on a whole different character.

2 cups all-purpose flour
2 teaspoons baking powder
¼ teaspoon salt
½ teaspoon ground ginger
½ teaspoon ground cloves
½ teaspoon ground nutmeg
2 large eggs, separated
½ cup (8 tablespoons) unsalted
    butter, softened to room
    temperature
½ cup sugar
1 cup buttermilk
1 cup seedless raisins
3 tablespoons chopped walnuts

1. Preheat oven to 375°F.

2. Sift flour, baking powder, salt, ginger, cloves, and nutmeg together into a bowl.

3. In a separate bowl, lightly beat egg yolks with a fork.

4. In a large mixing bowl, cream butter and sugar (beat until sugar is dissolved and mixture is creamy) with an electric mixer. Beat in buttermilk, then beaten egg yolks.

5. Stir in raisins and walnuts.

6. In a separate bowl, beat egg whites with an electric mixer until stiff (but not dry) peaks are formed.

7. Add flour mixture to wet ingredients in large mixing bowl and blend with a wooden spoon. Using a slotted spoon, gently fold in beaten egg whites.

8. Pour mixture into a greased and floured (bottom and sides dusted with flour) 9¼-inch loaf pan. Bake 45 to 55 minutes, until loaf begins to separate from the edges of the pan and a tester inserted into the center comes out clean.

Makes 1 loaf

BRANDIED SWEET POTATO BREAD

The taste of this luscious bread is sort of like a bite of sweet potato pie and a swig of rich, hearty brandy. Talk about southern comfort!

1½ cups all-purpose flour
1 tablespoon baking powder
1 teaspoon baking soda
1 teaspoon salt
1 tablespoon sugar
1 cup cooked, peeled, and
    mashed sweet potato
2 tablespoons brandy
2 large eggs, well beaten
½ cup sour cream
¼ cup milk
¼ cup (4 tablespoons) unsalted
    butter, melted
½ cup seedless golden raisins

1. Preheat oven to 375°F.

2. Sift flour, baking powder, baking soda, salt, and sugar together into a bowl.

3. Put sweet potato, brandy, and beaten eggs into a large mixing bowl. Beat with an electric mixer. Add sour cream and milk, mixing well. Add melted butter and beat until smooth.

4. Stir raisins into flour mixture. Add to the beaten ingredients in the large mixing bowl and blend well with a wooden spoon.

5. Pour mixture into a greased and floured (bottom and sides dusted with flour) 9¼-inch loaf pan. Bake 40 to 45 minutes, until loaf begins to separate from the edges of the pan and a tester inserted into the center comes out clean.

Makes 1 loaf

POPOVER BREAD

Think of this bread as a giant, extra-rich Yorkshire pudding that can elegantly accompany a roast on your dinner table. It's also great with jam for breakfast. Timing is crucial here. Be sure to have all ingredients in easy reach and follow the steps quickly. Serve this popover immediately for the full visual effect (it will deflate like a soufflé when you cut into it).

2 tablespoons olive oil
1 cup all-purpose flour
½ teaspoon salt
⅛ teaspoon cayenne pepper
3 large eggs
1 cup half and half
2 tablespoons unsalted butter,
    melted

1. Put olive oil in a 7-inch Pyrex casserole dish and place in oven. Preheat to 450°F.

2. Put flour, salt, and cayenne pepper into a sifter. Set aside.

3. In a large mixing bowl, beat eggs with an electric mixer. While continuing to beat, pour in half and half. Beating constantly, sift flour mixture directly into bowl. Add melted butter in a thin stream while still beating.

4. Remove heated casserole from oven. Carefully swirl oil to coat evenly. Quickly pour batter into casserole and immediately return the casserole to the oven. Bake 15 minutes. Reduce heat to 400°F and bake another 20 minutes. Serve immediately.

Makes 1 loaf

CLASSIC SPOONBREAD

Although it's not exactly a bread in the conventional sense, we've included a recipe for spoonbread here anyway. It's good, it's nourishing, it's easy to make, and it's a bit of a novelty.

2 cups milk
½ teaspoon salt
1 cup yellow cornmeal
1 teaspoon unsalted butter
2 teaspoons baking powder
4 large eggs, well beaten

1. Preheat oven to 400°F.

2. Combine milk and salt in a saucepan. Bring to a boil over medium heat. Reduce heat to low and stir in cornmeal. Continue to cook, stirring constantly, until mixture begins to thicken. Add butter and remove from heat.

3. Whisk in baking powder, then beaten eggs.

4. Pour mixture into a greased 7-inch round Pyrex casserole. Bake 40 to 45 minutes, until bread turns golden.

Makes 1 loaf

FRESH HERB BREAD

Summer-fresh rosemary, oregano, and thyme provide the savory flavor in this easy-to-make treat. Fresh herbs often are available in the produce section of many supermarkets and they're a must *for this bread.*

BREAD
2½ cups all-purpose flour
2½ teaspoons baking powder
½ teaspoon baking soda
½ teaspoon salt
1 teaspoon sugar
2 large eggs
½ cup buttermilk

TOPPING
½ cup (8 tablespoons) unsalted
   butter, melted
1 tablespoon chopped fresh
   rosemary
1 tablespoon chopped fresh
   oregano
1 tablespoon chopped fresh
   thyme

1. Preheat oven to 350°F.

2. Sift flour, baking powder, baking soda, salt, and sugar together into a bowl.

3. In a large mixing bowl, beat eggs until frothy with an electric mixer. While continuing to beat, add buttermilk.

4. Add flour mixture and blend thoroughly with a wooden spoon.

5. Pour into a greased and floured (bottom and sides dusted with flour) 9¼-inch loaf pan. With a sharp knife, make a slight incision most of the way down the middle of the dough. Bake for 20 minutes.

6. Toward the end of this baking cycle, mix melted butter and herbs. Using a well-insulated pot holder, carefully remove loaf pan from oven. Deepen slit down middle of dough (or cut new slit if incision has closed). Slowly pour butter mixture into slit, allowing bread to absorb as much as possible. With a pastry brush, paint the top of the loaf with remaining mixture. Bake another 15 to 20 minutes, until loaf begins to separate from the edges of the pan and a tester inserted into the center comes out clean.

Makes 1 loaf

SPINACH FETA CHEESE LOAF

This delicious Greek bread was inspired by our recent visit to Chicago's famous Parthenon restaurant, where the ouzo flows freely and flaming cheese is served with a resounding "Opaa!" (which means, we think, "Don't try this at home, kids"). Serve this bread with a bottle of good, strong, red wine.

BREAD
1 tablespoon olive oil
⅓ cup chopped white onion
2 garlic cloves, crushed
1 10-ounce package frozen
    chopped spinach, thawed,
    drained, excess water
    squeezed out
1 large egg
⅔ cup milk
¼ cup (4 tablespoons) unsalted
    butter, melted
2¼ cups all-purpose flour
1 tablespoon baking powder
½ teaspoon salt
½ teaspoon sugar
½ cup crumbled feta cheese

TOPPING
1 egg beaten with 1 tablespoon
    water to paint dough

1. Preheat oven to 350°F.

2. In a skillet, heat oil. Add onion and garlic. Cook over medium heat for about 1 minute, until onion begins to wilt. Add spinach and continue to cook until spinach looks dry (about 2 minutes). Remove from heat and set aside.

3. In a large mixing bowl, beat egg. Whisk in milk, then melted butter. Sift flour, baking powder, salt, and sugar together directly into the mixture. Mix with a wooden spoon until a ball of dough is formed.

4. Transfer dough to a 1½- to 2-foot-long sheet of wax paper. Lay a second sheet of wax paper on top of the dough. Using a rolling pin, flatten and shape dough to form an oblong about ½ inch thick. Remove the top sheet.

5. Spread spinach mixture lengthwise over bottom third of the flattened dough, leaving a ¼-inch border. Top with a layer of cheese.

6. Raise the left-hand side of the wax paper and fold dough about two-thirds of the way over onto itself, taking care not to force the filling out. Fold right-hand side over, then crimp ends to completely enclose filling. (The entire process is rather like folding a burrito.)

7. Carefully turn dough over and place seam side down, tucking ends under, on a greased cookie sheet that has been dusted with flour. Paint exposed surface of dough with egg and water mixture, using a pastry brush. With a sharp knife, make 2 slight diagonal incisions on top of dough (each about a third of the way along loaf). Bake 25 to 30 minutes, until a tester inserted into the side of the loaf comes out clean. Serve hot.

Makes 1 loaf

CHEDDAR DILL BREAD

Pungent dill adds just the right accent to this bread, while whole-wheat flour provides a hearty texture. Paired with an appetizer or salad, it's perfect as a quick, light meal.

1½ cups all-purpose flour
½ cup whole-wheat flour
1½ teaspoons baking powder
½ teaspoon baking soda
¼ teaspoon salt
4 teaspoons sugar
1 tablespoon dried dill
1 large egg
¼ cup (4 tablespoons) unsalted
    butter, melted
⅔ cup buttermilk
1 cup grated cheddar cheese

1. Preheat oven to 350°F.

2. Sift flours, baking powder, baking soda, salt, sugar, and dill together into a large mixing bowl.

3. Using an electric mixer, beat egg well. While continuing to beat, add melted butter and buttermilk. Stir in cheddar cheese.

4. Add liquid mixture to the flour mixture and blend with a wooden spoon.

5. Pour mixture into a greased and floured (bottom and sides dusted with flour) 9¼-inch loaf pan. Bake 40 to 50 minutes, until loaf begins to separate from the edges of the pan and a tester inserted into the center comes out clean.

Makes 1 loaf

DIXIE CORNBREAD WITH BACON

This is a crumbly down-home cornbread that derives its distinctive character from the bacon. The heartier and more flavorful the bacon you use, the better this cornbread will be.

1½ cups white cornmeal
¼ cup all-purpose flour
2 teaspoons baking powder
¼ teaspoon salt
1 tablespoon sugar
6 strips bacon
2 large eggs
1½ cups buttermilk
2 tablespoons vegetable oil

1. Preheat oven to 450°F.

2. Sift cornmeal, flour, baking powder, and salt together into a large mixing bowl. Mix in sugar.

3. Arrange bacon so that edges do not overlap in a heavy-bottomed 10-inch skillet (preferably a cast-iron skillet) with an ovenproof handle. Cook over medium heat until bacon turns translucent and edges begin to curl. Turn bacon over and cook other side just until pink and slightly firm, taking care not to brown it. Remove from heat, but do not drain.

4. Beat eggs well. Whisk buttermilk into beaten eggs until mixture turns a lemon hue. Whisk in vegetable oil. Add to the cornmeal/flour mixture and blend well with a wooden spoon until free of lumps.

5. Pour mixture into skillet over the bacon and place in oven. Bake 16 to 18 minutes, until edges of cornbread are deep brown and center is golden. After removing cornbread from oven, flip onto a serving plate so that the bacon-encrusted side is on top. Serve hot.

Makes 1 loaf

CHEDDAR CHEESE CORNBREAD

Paired with soup or a salad, this cornbread makes a quick and filling meal. We recommend using an extra-sharp cheddar to add some bite.

1⅓ cups yellow cornmeal
⅔ cup all-purpose flour
1 tablespoon baking powder
1 teaspoon salt
¼ teaspoon dried red pepper
   flakes
1 teaspoon ground coriander
1 cup sour cream
⅓ cup half and half
2 large eggs, well beaten
¼ cup (4 tablespoons) unsalted
   butter, melted
1½ cups grated extra-sharp
   cheddar cheese

1. Preheat oven to 425°F.

2. Sift cornmeal, flour, baking powder, and salt together into a bowl. Mix in red pepper flakes and coriander.

3. In a large mixing bowl, whisk sour cream and half and half together well. Add beaten eggs and whisk in thoroughly. Whisk in melted butter. Stir in cheese. Add cornmeal/flour mixture and blend well with a wooden spoon.

4. Pour mixture into a well-greased 9-inch round baking pan. Bake 20 to 25 minutes, until edges begin to brown. Serve hot.

Makes 1 loaf

DARK ZUCCHINI BREAD

This is an excellent dinner bread, especially for those who need some coaxing to eat their vegetables. A small amount of cocoa makes the bread richer, but not too sweet. Shred the zucchini in a food processor or by hand, using the large holes on a grater.

1 cup shredded zucchini, excess water squeezed out (about 2 medium or 1½ large zucchini)
¾ cup buttermilk
2 large eggs, well beaten
¼ cup vegetable oil
2½ cups all-purpose flour
1 teaspoon baking powder
½ teaspoon baking soda
½ teaspoon salt
¼ cup unsweetened cocoa powder, plus 1 tablespoon to dust pan
¼ cup sugar
½ teaspoon ground ginger
¼ teaspoon ground mace
¼ teaspoon ground nutmeg
½ cup seedless raisins

1. Preheat oven to 350°F.

2. Combine zucchini, buttermilk, beaten eggs, and vegetable oil. Mix well.

3. Sift flour, baking powder, baking soda, salt, and cocoa powder together into a large mixing bowl. Mix in sugar, ginger, mace, nutmeg, and raisins. Add liquid mixture and blend well with a wooden spoon.

4. Pour mixture into a well-greased 9¼-inch loaf pan that has been dusted (bottom and sides) with cocoa powder. Bake 45 to 55 minutes, until loaf begins to separate from the edges of the pan and a tester inserted into the center comes out clean.

Makes 1 loaf

PORT WINE AND FIG BREAD

We suggest using a good imported port for this sophisticated bread, which is definitely a grown-up taste treat. For a real pleasure, indulge yourself in a glass of the port along with the bread.

1½ cups chopped dried figs
   (stems removed)
¼ cup tawny port wine
2½ cups all-purpose flour
3½ teaspoons baking powder
¾ teaspoon baking soda
¼ teaspoon salt
¾ cup sugar
1 large egg
1 cup buttermilk
1 tablespoon unsalted butter,
   melted
½ cup chopped walnuts

1. Preheat oven to 350°F.

2. Mix figs and port wine in a small bowl and set aside.

3. Sift flour, baking powder, baking soda, salt, and sugar together into a large mixing bowl.

4. In a separate bowl, beat egg well with an electric mixer. Beat in buttermilk and melted butter. Mix until frothy.

5. Add to dry ingredients. Blend with a wooden spoon. Fold in figs and walnuts.

6. Pour mixture into a greased and floured (bottom and sides dusted with flour) 9¼-inch loaf pan. Bake 50 to 60 minutes, until loaf begins to separate from the edges of the pan and a tester inserted into the center comes out clean.

Makes 1 loaf

CROQUE MONSIEUR LOAF

You could call it "ham and cheese loaf," but this bread is so sublime it really does deserve its fashionably French name.

BREAD
1 large egg
⅔ cup milk
¼ cup (4 tablespoons) unsalted
    butter, melted
2 cups all-purpose flour
1 tablespoon baking powder
½ teaspoon salt

½ teaspoon sugar
2 tablespoons Dijon mustard
6 slices imported ham (about
    1 6-ounce package)
1 cup shredded Swiss cheese

TOPPING
1 beaten egg to paint dough

1. Preheat oven to 350°F.

2. In a large mixing bowl, beat egg. Whisk in milk, then melted butter. Sift flour, baking powder, salt, and sugar together directly into the mixture. Mix with a wooden spoon until a ball of dough is formed.

3. Transfer dough to a 1½- to 2-inch-long sheet of wax paper. Lay a second sheet of wax paper on top of the dough. Using a rolling pin, flatten and shape dough to form an oblong about ½ inch thick. Remove the top sheet. Coat the dough with mustard. Cover with a layer of ham, leaving a ½-inch border. Top with a layer of cheese.

4. Raise the left-hand side of the wax paper and fold dough about two-thirds of the way over onto itself, taking care not to force the filling out. Fold right-hand side over, then crimp ends to completely enclose filling.

5. Turn dough over and place seam side down, tucking ends under, on a greased and flour-dusted cookie sheet. Paint exposed surface of dough with beaten egg. Make 2 slight diagonal incisions on top of dough (each about a third of the way along loaf). Bake 25 to 30 minutes, until a tester inserted into the side comes out clean.

Makes 1 loaf

4
SWEET BREADS

◆

APPLESAUCE NUT BREAD

We used to turn up our noses at commercially prepared applesauce until we tried some of the new natural varieties and discovered how tasty they are. With this ingredient as well as nuts, brown sugar, and spices, this bread is reminiscent of an old-fashioned apple crisp or cobbler.

1 cup natural, unsweetened,
    chunky applesauce
½ cup pure clover honey
1 large egg, well beaten
¼ cup (4 tablespoons) unsalted
    butter, melted
2 cups all-purpose flour
2 tablespoons baking powder
¾ teaspoon baking soda
¼ teaspoon salt
⅓ cup dark brown sugar, firmly
    packed
½ teaspoon ground cloves
½ teaspoon ground cinnamon
½ teaspoon ground nutmeg
⅔ cup chopped pecans
⅓ cup seedless raisins

1. Preheat oven to 350°F.

2. In a large mixing bowl, combine applesauce, honey, beaten egg, and melted butter. Mix thoroughly.

3. Sift flour, baking powder, baking soda, salt, brown sugar, and spices together directly into the applesauce mixture. Mix with a wooden spoon just until blended. Fold in pecans and raisins.

4. Pour mixture into a greased and floured (bottom and sides dusted with flour) 9¼-inch loaf pan. Bake 40 to 50 minutes, until loaf begins to separate from the edges of the pan and a tester inserted into the center comes out clean.

Makes 1 loaf

BOBBI'S RAISIN RUM TEA BREAD

We thought we should dedicate this yummy bread to our friend Bobbi, who was in from California the weekend when we came up with the recipe. Poor Bobbi had to nibble her way through several variations before we were finally satisfied. Come to think of it, she wasn't exactly complaining. . . .

1¼ cups seedless raisins
2 cups all-purpose flour,
    divided into ¼-cup and
    1¾-cup measures
4 ounces rum (preferably light),
    divided in half
1½ teaspoons cream of tartar
1½ teaspoons baking soda
½ cup (8 tablespoons) unsalted
    butter, softened to room
    temperature
½ cup sugar
2 large eggs, well beaten
2 teaspoons vanilla extract
2 teaspoons almond extract

1. Preheat oven to 350°F.

2. Mix raisins with ¼ cup of the flour. A handful at a time, finely grind floured raisins in a food processor, until small balls are formed. Place in a small bowl, mix well with 2 ounces of the rum, and set aside.

3. Sift remaining 1¾ cups flour, cream of tartar, and baking soda together into a bowl.

4. In a large mixing bowl, cream butter with an electric mixer (beat until creamy). Add sugar and beat until completely dissolved. While continuing to beat, add beaten eggs. (Batter will have a curdlike consistency at this stage.) Add remaining 2 ounces of rum and extracts.

5. Stir in raisin mixture thoroughly. Add flour mixture and blend well with a wooden spoon.

6. Pour mixture into a greased and floured (bottom and sides dusted with flour) 9¼-inch loaf pan. Bake 35 to 45 minutes, until loaf begins to separate from the edges of the pan and a tester inserted into the center comes out clean.

Makes 1 loaf

RHUBARB BREAD

We lovers of fresh rhubarb delight in every new culinary innovation for its use. For a truly intense rhubarb flavor, spread rhubarb jam on this bread.

1½ cups all-purpose flour
1 teaspoon baking soda
¾ teaspoon baking powder
¼ teaspoon salt
⅔ cup dark brown sugar, firmly
    packed
1½ teaspoons ground cinnamon
1 teaspoon ground allspice
1 large egg
½ cup vegetable oil
1 teaspoon vanilla extract
1½ cups chopped rhubarb
    (unpeeled)
½ cup golden seedless raisins

1. Preheat oven to 350°F.

2. Sift flour, baking soda, baking powder, salt, brown sugar, cinnamon, and allspice together into a large mixing bowl.

3. In a separate bowl, whisk egg until well beaten. Whisk in oil and vanilla.

4. Add to the flour mixture and blend with a wooden spoon. Fold in rhubarb and raisins.

5. Pour mixture into a greased and floured (bottom and sides dusted with flour) 9¼-inch loaf pan. Bake 45 to 55 minutes, until loaf begins to separate from the edges of the pan and a tester inserted into the center comes out clean.

Makes 1 loaf

MAPLE WALNUT FIG BREAD

We've found that this intense bread is even better the day after it's baked, when its distinct flavors have had time to meld.

1 large egg
½ cup milk
½ cup pure maple syrup
¼ cup (4 tablespoons) unsalted
    butter, melted
2 cups all-purpose flour
2 teaspoons baking powder
½ teaspoon salt
½ cup chopped walnuts
¾ cup coarsely chopped dried
    figs (stems removed)

1. Preheat oven to 375°F.

2. Using an electric mixer, beat egg well in a large mixing bowl. Add milk, maple syrup, and melted butter. Mix thoroughly.

3. Sift flour, baking powder, and salt together directly into liquid mixture. Blend thoroughly with a wooden spoon. Stir in walnuts and figs.

4. Pour mixture into a greased 9¼-inch loaf pan. Bake 40 to 50 minutes, until loaf begins to separate from the edges of the pan and a tester inserted into the center comes out clean.

Makes 1 loaf

MANDARIN ORANGE NUT BREAD

Here's a tasty teatime treat. We like to use this recipe to make muffins for late-night snacking, too. Orange butter is a wonderful accompaniment to this bread—simply soften one stick of butter, add about 2 teaspoons of grated fresh orange zest and about 2 tablespoons of juice from the mandarin oranges, and whip.

BREAD
2½ cups all-purpose flour
2 teaspoons baking powder
½ teaspoon salt
2 tablespoons unsalted butter,
    melted
½ cup milk
½ cup sugar
2 large eggs
½ cup chopped walnuts
1 11-ounce can mandarin
    orange sections, drained,
    liquid reserved

GLAZE
¼ cup liquid from mandarin
    oranges
¼ cup sugar

1. Preheat oven to 375°F.

2. Sift flour, baking powder, and salt together into a bowl.

3. In a large mixing bowl, mix melted butter, milk, and sugar. Beat with an electric mixer until sugar is dissolved. While continuing to beat, add eggs one at a time.

4. Add the flour mixture and blend well with a wooden spoon. Stir in nuts and mandarin orange sections.

5. Pour into a greased and floured (bottom and sides dusted with flour) 9¼-inch loaf pan. Bake 45 to 55 minutes, until loaf begins to separate from the edges of the pan and a tester inserted into the center comes out clean.

6. For glaze, combine reserved mandarin orange liquid and sugar in a small saucepan. Cook over medium heat, stirring constantly until sugar is dissolved. Bring to a boil, then lower heat to simmer. Cook about 10 minutes more, until a thick syrup is formed. Pour over bread that has cooled. Allow glaze to cool and harden on bread for a few minutes before serving.

Makes 1 loaf

STRAWBERRY CHEESE LOAF

This bread has something sure to please almost any sweet tooth. In addition to the namesake fruit and cheese filling, the sweet nutty taste of almonds flavors the dough. It's equally good for breakfast or dessert.

BREAD
⅓ cup buttermilk
½ cup sour cream
2 large eggs, well beaten
2¼ cups all-purpose flour (you may need to add 1–2 additional tablespoons when shaping dough), plus 2 tablespoons to roll dough ball in
2½ teaspoons baking powder
¾ teaspoon baking soda
¼ teaspoon salt
¼ cup sugar
6 ounces cream cheese (2 3-ounce packages or ¾ of 1 8-ounce package), softened to room temperature

¼ cup milk
¾ cup strawberry spreadable fruit
2 teaspoons vanilla extract
¼ cup blanched slivered almonds

TOPPING
2 tablespoons milk to paint dough
2 teaspoons sugar mixed with ¼ teaspoon ground mace

1. Preheat oven to 350°F.

2. Place buttermilk and sour cream in a large mixing bowl and beat with an electric mixer. Mix in beaten eggs.

3. Sift flour, baking powder, baking soda, salt, and sugar together directly into mixture.

4. Mix with a wooden spoon until crumbly. With lightly floured hands, form dough into a ball (adding 1–2 tablespoons flour if needed).

5. Sprinkle 2 tablespoons flour onto a 1½- to 2-foot-long sheet of wax paper. Transfer dough to wax paper and roll until covered with flour. Lay a second sheet of wax paper on top of the dough and press down with your hand to spread dough evenly until about ½ inch thick. Remove the top sheet of wax paper.

6. Whisk cream cheese and milk together until well blended. Whisk in spreadable fruit and vanilla extract. Spread mixture lengthwise over the middle third of the flattened dough, leaving a slight border on each side. Sprinkle almonds on top.

7. Raise the bottom of the wax paper and fold dough about halfway up onto itself, taking care not to force the filling out. Fold top side down just enough to overlap, then crimp the ends to completely enclose filling.

8. Carefully turn dough over and place seam side down, tucking ends under, on a greased cookie sheet that has been dusted with flour. Brush off any excess flour residue on dough. Paint exposed surface of dough with milk, using a pastry brush. Sprinkle sugar and mace mixture over the top. With a sharp knife, make a slight incision most of the way down the middle of the dough. Bake 25 to 30 minutes, until a tester inserted into the side of the loaf comes out clean.

9. When done, let cool slightly on cookie sheet. (Do not attempt to transfer to a cooling rack, as the loaf could crack.) Serve warm or reheat in a microwave oven set at full power for about 30 seconds.

Makes 1 loaf

STRAWBERRY WALNUT BREAD

Here's a comfort food with a cool hint of summer to take the edge off a cruel winter's day. We call for frozen strawberries so that you can enjoy this bread all year 'round. (As we call for very little other liquid, the water remaining in the strawberries after thawing will be just enough to make the bread moist.)

1 cup frozen sliced strawberries
2 large eggs
½ cup vegetable oil
1 teaspoon vanilla extract
2 cups all-purpose flour
1 teaspoon baking soda
¼ teaspoon salt
¾ cup sugar
1 tablespoon ground cinnamon
¾ cup chopped walnuts

1. Preheat oven to 375°F.

2. Place frozen strawberries in a colander and set aside in sink or over a bowl. Let strawberries completely thaw and drain.

3. In a large mixing bowl, beat eggs well with a wire whisk. Whisk in oil, then vanilla.

4. Sift flour, baking soda, salt, sugar, and cinnamon together directly into egg mixture. Blend with a wooden spoon. Gently fold in thawed and drained strawberries. Mix in nuts.

5. Pour mixture into a greased and floured (bottom and sides dusted with flour) 9¼-inch loaf pan. Bake 45 to 55 minutes, until loaf begins to separate from the edges of the pan and a tester inserted into the center comes out clean.

Makes 1 loaf

LEMON POPPY SEED TEA BREAD

It's "two for tea and tea for two" according to the lyric. In this recipe, two well-matched flavors, lemon and poppy seed, pair off in a rich and creamy tea bread.

1½ cups all-purpose flour
1½ teaspoons baking powder
½ teaspoon salt
½ cup (8 tablespoons) unsalted
    butter, softened to room
    temperature
1 cup sugar
½ cup buttermilk
2 large eggs, well beaten
½ tablespoon grated lemon rind
2 teaspoons poppy seeds
3 tablespoons freshly squeezed
    lemon juice

1. Preheat oven to 350°F.

2. Sift flour, baking powder, and salt together into a bowl.

3. In a large mixing bowl, cream butter and sugar (beat until sugar has dissolved and mixture is creamy) with an electric mixer. Beat in buttermilk, then beaten eggs.

4. Add flour mixture and blend well with a wooden spoon. Stir in lemon rind and poppy seeds. Add lemon juice and mix well.

5. Pour mixture into a greased and floured (bottom and sides dusted with flour) 9¼-inch loaf pan. Bake 45 to 55 minutes, until loaf begins to separate from the edges of the pan and a tester inserted into the center comes out clean.

Makes 1 loaf

RASPBERRY CINNAMON SWIRL

If this recipe sounds a bit like rugelach *to you, you're right. This sweet bread is indebted to the classic Jewish cream cheese treat from which it is derived.*

2¼ cups all-purpose flour
2¼ teaspoons baking powder
¾ teaspoon baking soda
½ teaspoon salt
3 tablespoons sugar, plus
    2 tablespoons mixed with
    2 teaspoons cinnamon to
    roll dough ball in
1 3-ounce package cream
    cheese, softened to room
    temperature
¼ cup milk
2 large eggs, well beaten
2 tablespoons unsalted butter,
    melted
½ cup raspberry spreadable fruit
⅓ cup crushed walnuts
¼ cup seedless raisins

1. Preheat oven to 350°F.

2. Sift flour, baking powder, baking soda, salt, and sugar together into a bowl.

3. In a large mixing bowl, cream the cream cheese and milk (beat until well blended and creamy) with an electric mixer. While continuing to beat, add beaten eggs. Beat in melted butter until mixture is frothy.

4. Add flour mixture and stir with a wooden spoon until a ball of dough is formed.

5. Sprinkle sugar and cinnamon mixture onto a 1½- to 2-foot-long sheet of wax paper. Transfer dough to wax paper and roll until covered. Press down with your hand and spread dough evenly into an oblong about 1 foot long and ¼ inch thick, working as much of the remaining coating as possible into the dough.

6. Layer spreadable fruit over dough, leaving about a ½-inch border. Scatter walnuts and raisins on top, packing down gently into the spreadable fruit.

7. Raise the left-hand side of the wax paper and fold dough continuously over onto itself to form a log, incorporating any loose coating remaining on the wax paper. Crimp the ends.

8. Place seam side down on a greased cookie sheet that has been dusted with flour, tucking ends under. With a sharp knife, make a slight incision most of the way down the middle of the dough. Bake 25 to 30 minutes, until a tester inserted into the side of the loaf comes out clean. Remove from oven carefully, as cookie sheet will be very hot.

Makes 1 loaf

MARCIA JO'S PEAR BRANDY AND HONEY BREAD

We love the strong but elegant flavor of pear brandy. So does our friend Marcia Jo, who finds almost any excuse to incorporate it into a new recipe.

1 cup sugar
½ cup (8 tablespoons) unsalted
    butter, softened to room
    temperature
2 large eggs, well beaten
¼ cup buttermilk
¼ cup pure clover honey
1 teaspoon vanilla extract
¼ cup pear brandy
2 cups all-purpose flour
1 teaspoon baking powder
½ teaspoon baking soda
½ teaspoon salt
¼ teaspoon ground nutmeg
1 cup unpeeled, cored, coarsely
    chopped pear

1. Preheat oven to 350°F.

2. Using an electric mixer, cream sugar and softened butter (beat until sugar is dissolved and mixture is creamy). While continuing to beat, slowly add eggs.

3. Whisk in buttermilk, honey, vanilla, and brandy. Mix well.

4. Sift flour, baking powder, baking soda, salt, and nutmeg together into a large mixing bowl. Add liquid mixture and blend with a wooden spoon. Gently fold in chopped pear.

5. Pour mixture into a greased and floured (bottom and sides dusted with flour) 9¼-inch loaf pan. Bake 50 to 60 minutes, until loaf begins to separate from the edges of the pan and a tester inserted into the center comes out clean.

Makes 1 loaf

PEAR MANGO BREAD

Light and fruity, this quick bread is sure to make a tasty impression at either the breakfast or the dinner table. Mango nectar is readily available in the canned juice section of most supermarkets.

2½ cups all-purpose flour
2 teaspoons baking powder
½ teaspoon salt
¼ cup (4 tablespoons) unsalted
    butter, melted
1 cup mango nectar
½ cup sugar
2 large eggs
1 16-ounce can pears, drained
    and coarsely chopped

1. Preheat oven to 375°F.

2. Sift flour, baking powder, and salt together into a bowl.

3. In a large mixing bowl, mix melted butter, mango nectar, and sugar. Beat with an electric mixer until sugar is dissolved. While continuing to beat, add eggs one at a time.

4. Add the flour mixture and blend well with a wooden spoon. Stir in chopped pears.

5. Pour into a greased and floured (bottom and sides dusted with flour) 9¼-inch loaf pan. Bake 45 to 55 minutes, until loaf begins to separate from the edges of the pan and a tester inserted into the center comes out clean.

Makes 1 loaf

PAPAYA FILBERT BREAD

The combination of two distinctly flavored, unusual ingredients makes for one superlative quick bread here. Papaya nectar is found canned in the juice section of supermarkets. In some areas of the country, filberts are also called hazelnuts.

2½ cups all-purpose flour
2 teaspoons baking powder
½ teaspoon salt
¼ cup (4 tablespoons) unsalted
    butter, melted
1 cup papaya nectar
½ cup dark brown sugar, firmly
    packed
2 large eggs
¾ cup chopped, toasted filberts

1. Preheat oven to 375°F.

2. Sift flour, baking powder, and salt together into a bowl.

3. In a large mixing bowl, mix melted butter, papaya nectar, and sugar. Beat with an electric mixer until sugar is dissolved. While continuing to beat, add eggs one at a time.

4. Add the flour mixture and blend well with a wooden spoon. Stir in chopped filberts.

5. Pour into a greased and floured (bottom and sides dusted with flour) 9¼-inch loaf pan. Bake 45 to 55 minutes, until loaf begins to separate from the edges of the pan and a tester inserted into the center comes out clean.

Note: To toast filberts, place the nuts in a single layer on a cookie sheet. Broil, about 2 inches from heat, for 2–3 minutes until nuts are golden brown.

Makes 1 loaf

CRANBERRY APRICOT LOAF

Remember that fresh cranberries are often scarce during the year—stock up and freeze them in the fall so that you can enjoy this treat all year 'round.

2⅓ cups all-purpose flour
2 teaspoons baking powder
½ teaspoon salt
⅓ cup (5⅓ tablespoons) unsalted butter, softened to room temperature
⅔ cup sugar
2 large eggs
½ cup milk
⅔ cup apricot spreadable fruit
1 cup cranberries

1. Preheat oven to 375°F.

2. Sift flour, baking powder, and salt together into a bowl.

3. In a large mixing bowl, cream butter and sugar (beat until well blended and creamy) with an electric mixer. Beat in eggs one at a time. Beat in milk.

4. Mix in spreadable fruit with a wooden spoon. Add flour mixture and blend well. Stir in cranberries.

5. Pour mixture into a greased and floured (bottom and sides dusted with flour) 9¼-inch loaf pan. Bake 50 to 55 minutes, until loaf begins to separate from the edges of the pan and a tester inserted into the center comes out clean.

Makes 1 loaf

PUMPKIN PIE BREAD

Here's a tasty alternative to the traditional Thanksgiving pie, and making it is easier than . . . you know what. Try it toasted on chilly winter mornings, too.

1 8-ounce can solid-pack
   pumpkin
½ cup vegetable oil
¼ cup water
2 large eggs, well beaten
2 cups all-purpose flour
1 teaspoon baking soda
¼ teaspoon salt
1½ cups sugar
1 teaspoon ground cinnamon
1 teaspoon ground allspice
½ teaspoon ground cloves

1. Preheat oven to 350°F.

2. In a large mixing bowl, beat pumpkin, oil, water, and beaten eggs together with an electric mixer until creamy.

3. Sift flour, baking soda, salt, sugar, and spices together directly into the liquid mixture. Using a wooden spoon, mix just until blended.

4. Pour mixture into a greased and floured (bottom and sides dusted with flour) 9¼-inch loaf pan. Bake 50 to 60 minutes, until loaf begins to separate from the edges of the pan and a tester inserted into the center comes out clean.

Makes 1 loaf

DOOR COUNTY SOUR CHERRY BREAD

Door County, Wisconsin, produces some of the finest sour cherries to be had, and the "need to stock up on sour cherries" has more than once provided us with a viable excuse to visit the woodsy peninsula.

BREAD
⅓ cup buttermilk
¾ cup sour cream, divided into
    ½-cup and ¼-cup measures
2 large eggs, well beaten
2¼ cups all-purpose flour (you
    may need to add 1 to 2
    additional tablespoons
    when shaping dough), plus
    2 tablespoons to roll dough
    ball in
2½ teaspoons baking powder
¾ teaspoon baking soda
¼ teaspoon salt
¼ cup sugar

1 3-ounce package cream
    cheese, softened to room
    temperature
¼ cup milk
2 tablespoons dark brown sugar,
    firmly packed
⅛ teaspoon ground cardamom
1 cup pitted sour cherries (fresh
    or canned; drained if
    canned)

TOPPING
2 tablespoons milk to paint
    dough
2 teaspoons sugar

1. Preheat oven to 350°F.

2. Place buttermilk and ½ cup of the sour cream in a large mixing bowl and beat with an electric mixer. Mix in beaten eggs.

3. Sift flour, baking powder, baking soda, salt, and sugar together directly into mixture.

4. Mix with a wooden spoon until crumbly. With lightly floured hands, form dough into a ball (adding 1 to 2 tablespoons flour if needed).

5. Sprinkle 2 tablespoons flour onto a 1½- to 2-foot-long sheet of wax paper. Transfer dough to wax paper and roll until covered with flour. Lay a second sheet of wax paper on top of the dough and press down with your hand to spread dough evenly until it is about ¼ inch thick. Remove the top sheet of wax paper.

6. Whisk cream cheese, milk, and remaining ¼ cup of sour cream together until well blended. Add brown sugar and cardamom. Stir in sour cherries. Spread mixture lengthwise over the middle third of the flattened dough, leaving a slight border on each side.

7. Raise the bottom of the wax paper and fold dough about halfway up onto itself, taking care not to force the filling out. Fold top side down just enough to overlap, then crimp the ends to completely enclose filling.

8. Carefully turn dough over and place seam side down, tucking ends under, on a greased cookie sheet that has been dusted with flour. Brush off any excess flour residue on dough. Paint exposed surface of dough with milk, using a pastry brush. Sprinkle sugar over top. With a sharp knife, make a slight incision most of the way down the middle of the dough. Bake 25 to 30 minutes, until a tester inserted into the side of the loaf comes out clean.

9. Remove from oven and let cool slightly on cookie sheet to prevent loaf from cracking. Serve warm or reheat in a microwave oven set at full power for about 30 seconds.

Makes 1 loaf

ORANGE MARMALADE BREAD

Orange marmalade lends distinctive character to this bread—adding moisture, crunch, and zip!

1½ cups all-purpose flour
2 teaspoons baking powder
¼ teaspoon salt
½ cup sugar
1 large egg
½ cup orange marmalade
½ cup orange juice (preferably
    freshly squeezed)
4 teaspoons unsalted butter,
    melted
¾ cup golden seedless raisins

1. Preheat oven to 350°F.

2. Sift flour, baking powder, salt, and sugar together into a large mixing bowl.

3. In a separate bowl, beat egg well with an electric mixer. Mix in marmalade, orange juice, and melted butter.

4. Add to the flour mixture and blend with a wooden spoon. Fold in raisins.

5. Pour mixture into a greased and floured (bottom and sides dusted with flour) 9¼-inch loaf pan. Bake 50 to 60 minutes, until loaf begins to separate from the edges of the pan and a tester inserted into the center comes out clean.

Makes 1 loaf

BUTTERSCOTCH–BUTTERSCOTCH CHIP BREAD

A double delight! Just as you begin to savor the subtle richness of the butterscotch flavor in this bread, your teeth sink into the extra bliss of a butterscotch chip.

2 cups all-purpose flour
2¼ teaspoons baking powder
¾ teaspoon baking soda
¼ teaspoon salt
¼ cup (4 tablespoons) unsalted
    butter, softened to room
    temperature
⅔ cup dark brown sugar, firmly
    packed
1 large egg, well beaten
1 teaspoon vanilla extract
⅔ cup buttermilk
½ cup butterscotch chips

1. Preheat oven to 350°F.

2. Sift flour, baking powder, baking soda, and salt together into a bowl.

3. In a large mixing bowl, cream butter and brown sugar (beat until sugar is dissolved and mixture is creamy) with an electric mixer. Mix in beaten egg. Continuing to beat, add vanilla extract, then buttermilk.

4. Stir in butterscotch chips. Add flour mixture and blend well with a wooden spoon.

5. Pour mixture into a greased and floured (bottom and sides dusted with flour) 9¼-inch loaf pan. Bake 45 to 55 minutes, until loaf begins to separate from the edges of the pan and a tester inserted into the center comes out clean.

Makes 1 loaf

BUBBA'S POPPY SEED BREAD

We're definitely dealing with a comfort food here, albeit a "quick" rendition thereof. We think Grandma would approve of the execution as well as the sentiment.

BREAD
2 large eggs
⅔ cup buttermilk
2 tablespoons unsalted butter,
    melted
2¼ cups all-purpose flour, plus
    2 tablespoons to roll dough
    ball in
3¼ teaspoons baking powder
½ teaspoon salt
⅓ cup sugar
1 can (about 12 ounces) poppy
    seed filling
2 tablespoons hazelnut liqueur

TOPPING
1 egg beaten with 2 tablespoons
    water to paint dough

1. Preheat oven to 350°F.

2. In a large mixing bowl, beat eggs. Whisk in buttermilk, then melted butter. Sift flour, baking powder, salt, and sugar together directly into the mixture.

3. Mix with a wooden spoon until crumbly. With lightly floured hands, form dough into a ball, incorporating any dry ingredients remaining in the bowl into the dough.

4. Sprinkle 2 tablespoons of flour onto a 1½- to 2-foot-long sheet of wax paper. Transfer dough to wax paper and roll until covered with flour. Lay a second sheet of wax paper on top of the dough and press down with your hand to spread dough evenly until it is about ½ inch thick. Remove the top sheet of wax paper and any excess flour from the bottom sheet.

5. Mix poppy seed filling and liqueur in a small bowl and spread over the flattened dough, leaving a ½-inch border.

6. Raise the left-hand side of the wax paper and fold dough about two-thirds of the way over onto itself, taking care not to force the filling out. Fold right-hand side over, then crimp the ends to completely enclose filling.

7. Carefully turn dough over and place seam side down, tucking ends under, in a greased 9¼-inch loaf pan. Paint exposed surface of dough with egg and water mixture, using a pastry brush. Bake 50 to 55 minutes, until loaf begins to separate from the edges of the pan and a tester inserted into the center comes out clean.

Makes 1 loaf

JILL'S OATMEAL RAISIN BREAD

This recipe was inspired by our friend Jill's oatmeal-raisin cookie recipe. Serve this bread warm, with a tall glass of cold milk.

1½ cups dark raisins
½ cup very hot or boiling water
½ cup sugar
3 tablespoons unsalted butter,
    softened to room
    temperature
1½ cups rolled oats
1½ cups all-purpose flour
2 teaspoons baking powder
1½ teaspoons baking soda
½ teaspoon salt
2 large eggs
1 cup buttermilk
½ cup chopped walnuts

1. Preheat oven to 375°F.

2. Combine raisins, water, sugar, and butter. Mix until butter has melted and set aside.

3. Grind oats to a powdery consistency in a food processor or blender.

4. Sift flour, baking powder, baking soda, and salt together into a bowl. Mix in ground oats.

5. In a large mixing bowl, beat eggs well. Whisk in buttermilk. Stir in raisin mixture. Add flour-oat mixture and blend well with a wooden spoon. Stir in nuts.

6. Pour into a greased 9¼-inch loaf pan. Bake 50 to 55 minutes, until loaf begins to separate from the edges of the pan and a tester inserted into the center comes out clean.

Makes 1 loaf

ORANGE PECAN TEA BREAD

An orange glaze topping this loaf lends visual diversity to the breadbasket and a pleasant crunch to the palate. This is a dense, rich bread, best served thinly sliced—but be prepared to cut a lot of slices.

BREAD
2½ cups all-purpose flour
2 teaspoons baking powder
½ teaspoon salt
2 tablespoons unsalted butter, melted
1 tablespoon grated orange rind
1 cup orange juice (preferably freshly squeezed, with some pulp)

1 cup sugar
2 large eggs
¾ cup chopped pecans

TOPPING
½ cup cold water
¼ cup sugar
2 tablespoons finely chopped orange rind

1. Preheat oven to 375°F.

2. Sift flour, baking powder, and salt together into a bowl.

3. In a large mixing bowl, mix melted butter and orange rind well. Add orange juice and sugar. Beat with an electric mixer until sugar is dissolved. While continuing to beat, add eggs one at a time.

4. Add the flour mixture and blend well with a wooden spoon. Stir in pecans.

5. Pour mixture into a greased and floured (bottom and sides dusted with flour) 9¼-inch loaf pan. Bake 45 to 55 minutes, until loaf begins to separate from the edges of the pan and a tester inserted into the center comes out clean.

6. For glaze, combine water, sugar, and orange rind in a small saucepan. Cook over medium heat, stirring constantly, until sugar is dissolved. Bring to a boil, then reduce heat to simmer. Cook about 10 minutes more, until a thick syrup forms. Pour syrup over bread that has cooled. Allow glaze to cool and harden on bread for a few minutes before serving.

Makes 1 loaf

RASPBERRY MACADAMIA NUT DELIGHT

Two of life's most elegant little taste treats, raspberry and macadamia nut, team up to make this bread a very special antidote to life's frequent frustrations. Since we use raspberry preserves in the recipe, you don't even have to wait for fresh raspberries to come in season.

2 cups all-purpose flour
1½ teaspoons baking powder
½ teaspoon baking soda
¼ teaspoon salt
½ cup dark brown sugar, firmly packed
⅓ cup buttermilk

⅓ cup raspberry preserves
¼ cup (4 tablespoons) unsalted butter, melted
1 large egg, well beaten
1 cup roughly chopped macadamia nuts

1. Preheat oven to 375°F.

2. Sift flour, baking powder, baking soda, salt, and brown sugar together into a large mixing bowl.

3. In a separate bowl, whisk together buttermilk and raspberry preserves. Whisk in melted butter and beaten egg.

4. Add to the flour mixture and blend with a wooden spoon. Fold in macadamia nuts.

5. Pour mixture into a greased and floured (bottom and sides dusted with flour) 9¼-inch loaf pan. Bake 40 to 50 minutes, until loaf begins to separate from the edges of the pan and a tester inserted into the center comes out clean.

Makes 1 loaf

NUTTY MAPLE YOGURT BREAD

Yogurt gives this sweet bread a slightly tangy flavor and a supremely moist texture. Walnuts may be used instead of pecans if desired.

1 large egg
½ cup plain low-fat yogurt
½ cup pure maple syrup
¼ cup (4 tablespoons) unsalted
   butter, melted
2 cups all-purpose flour
2 teaspoons baking powder
½ teaspoon salt
1 cup chopped pecans

1. Preheat oven to 375°F.

2. Using an electric mixer, beat egg well in a large mixing bowl. Add yogurt, maple syrup, and melted butter. Mix thoroughly.

3. Sift flour, baking powder, and salt together directly into liquid mixture. Blend thoroughly with a wooden spoon. Stir in pecans.

4. Pour into a greased 9¼-inch loaf pan. Bake 40 to 50 minutes, until loaf begins to separate from the edges of the pan and a tester inserted into the center comes out clean.

Makes 1 loaf

APRICOT CREAM CHEESE SWIRL

This delightful sweet treat is really so easy to prepare that we think it may become a favorite accompaniment for your afternoon cup of tea.

2 large eggs
⅔ cup buttermilk
2 tablespoons unsalted butter,
    melted
2¼ cups all-purpose flour
3¼ teaspoons baking powder
½ teaspoon salt
⅓ cup sugar, plus 2 tablespoons
    mixed with ½ teaspoon
    ground cinnamon to roll
    dough ball in
1 3-ounce package cream
    cheese, softened to room
    temperature
1 tablespoon milk
¼ cup chopped dried apricots,
    tightly packed
¼ cup coarsely chopped walnuts

1. Preheat oven to 350°F.

2. In a large mixing bowl, beat eggs. Whisk in buttermilk, then melted butter. Sift flour, baking powder, salt, and sugar together directly into the mixture.

3. Mix with a wooden spoon until crumbly. With lightly floured hands, form dough into a ball, incorporating any dry ingredients remaining in the bowl into the dough.

4. Sprinkle the sugar and cinnamon mixture onto a 1½- to 2-foot-long sheet of wax paper. Transfer dough to wax paper and roll until covered. Lay a second sheet of wax paper on top of the dough and press down with your hand to spread dough evenly until it is about ½ inch thick. Remove the top sheet of wax paper.

5. Mix cream cheese and milk with a fork until creamy and spread over the flattened dough, leaving a ¼-inch border. Sprinkle apricots and walnuts on top.

6. Raise the left-hand side of the wax paper and roll dough continuously over onto itself to form a log, then crimp the ends.

7. Place seam side down in a greased 9¼-inch loaf pan, tucking ends under. Bake 50 to 55 minutes, until loaf begins to separate from the edges of the pan and a tester inserted into the center comes out clean.

Makes 1 loaf

CINNAMON RAISIN BREAD

In contrast to our more savory 1890s Raisin Spice Bread (see Index), this is the traditional raisin bread you probably remember as a childhood treat, full of sugar and cinnamon. It's great at breakfast and you can still enjoy it as a treat, even if you are a grown-up.

1 large egg
1 cup buttermilk
¼ cup (4 tablespoons) unsalted
    butter, melted
2½ cups all-purpose flour
2½ teaspoons baking powder
½ teaspoon baking soda
¼ teaspoon salt
½ cup sugar
½ cup dark brown sugar, firmly
    packed
1 tablespoon ground cinnamon
1 cup seedless raisins

1. Preheat oven to 350°F.

2. In a large mixing bowl, beat egg well with a wire whisk. Whisk in buttermilk and melted butter.

3. Sift flour, baking powder, baking soda, salt, sugar, brown sugar, and cinnamon together directly into the liquid mixture. Blend well with a wooden spoon. Fold in raisins.

4. Pour mixture into a greased and floured (bottom and sides dusted with flour) 9¼-inch loaf pan. Bake 45 to 55 minutes, until loaf begins to separate from the edges of the pan and a tester inserted into the center comes out clean.

Makes 1 loaf

NUTTY PRUNE BREAD

Prune Danish, step aside! We think this is an eminently lighter and tastier way for the prune lovers of the world to get their fix.

1½ cups coarsely chopped pitted prunes
½ cup very hot or boiling water
½ cup sugar
3 tablespoons unsalted butter, softened to room temperature
1½ cups rolled oats

1½ cups all-purpose flour
2 teaspoons baking powder
1½ teaspoons baking soda
½ teaspoon salt
2 large eggs
1 cup buttermilk
½ cup chopped walnuts

1. Preheat oven to 375°F.

2. Combine prunes, water, sugar, and butter. Mix until butter has melted and set aside.

3. Grind oats to a powdery consistency in a food processor or blender.

4. Sift flour, baking powder, baking soda, and salt together into a bowl. Mix in ground oats.

5. In a large mixing bowl, beat eggs well. Whisk in buttermilk. Stir in prune mixture. Add flour/oat mixture and blend well with a wooden spoon. Stir in walnuts.

6. Pour mixture into a greased 9¼-inch loaf pan. Bake 50 to 55 minutes, until loaf begins to separate from the edges of the pan and a tester inserted into the center comes out clean.

Makes 1 loaf

PINEAPPLE ZUCCHINI BREAD

This variation on the classic zucchini bread has a sunny hint of pineapple added to the traditional recipe.

1 small can crushed pineapple (about 8 ounces), drained well

1 cup shredded zucchini, excess water squeezed out (about 2 medium or 1½ large zucchini)

¾ cup buttermilk

2 large eggs, well beaten

¼ cup vegetable oil

2 tablespoons vanilla extract

2½ cups all-purpose flour

1 teaspoon baking powder

½ teaspoon baking soda

½ teaspoon salt

¼ cup sugar

2 teaspoons ground cinnamon

1 teaspoon ground nutmeg

½ cup dark seedless raisins

1. Preheat oven to 350°F.

2. Combine pineapple, zucchini, buttermilk, beaten eggs, vegetable oil, and vanilla extract. Mix well.

3. Sift flour, baking powder, baking soda, and salt together into a large mixing bowl. Mix in sugar, cinnamon, nutmeg, and raisins. Add liquid mixture and blend well with a wooden spoon.

4. Pour into a well-greased 9¼-inch loaf pan. Bake 45 to 55 minutes, until loaf begins to separate from the edges of the pan and a tester inserted into the center comes out clean.

Makes 1 loaf

LINDA'S CHOCOLATE CHIP CHEESECAKE BREAD

For our first book, we concocted a dip based on chocolate chip cheesecake, our friend Linda's favorite treat. Our latest variation on the theme of these well-matched flavors is a sinfully luscious dessert bread.

2½ cups all-purpose flour
2½ teaspoons baking powder
½ teaspoon salt
1 8-ounce package cream cheese, softened to room temperature
2 tablespoons brandy
½ teaspoon vanilla extract

½ cup milk
1 large egg, well beaten
¼ cup dark brown sugar, firmly packed
1 teaspoon ground cinnamon
½ cup mini chocolate chips
¼ cup coarsely chopped walnuts

1. Preheat oven to 375°F.

2. Sift flour, baking powder, and salt together into a bowl.

3. Place cream cheese, brandy, and vanilla extract into a large mixing bowl. Using an electric mixer, cream together (beat to a fluffy consistency). While continuing to beat, add milk, then beaten egg. Beat in brown sugar.

4. Stir in cinnamon, chocolate chips, and nuts. Add flour mixture and blend well with a wooden spoon.

5. Pour mixture into a greased 9¼-inch loaf pan. Bake 40 to 50 minutes, until loaf begins to separate from the edges of the pan and a tester inserted into the center comes out clean.

Makes 1 loaf

CLAUDIA'S APPLE CINNAMON SWIRL

This recipe was suggested by our friend Claudia, who liked Barry's apple pie so much she even ate it for breakfast. Here we've incorporated the same taste in a rich, creamy breakfast bread.

1 large Rome apple, peeled and
    cubed (about 1 firmly
    packed cup)
¾ teaspoon ground cinnamon
¼ teaspoon ground nutmeg
½ tablespoon freshly squeezed
    lemon juice
½ cup (8 tablespoons) unsalted
    butter, softened to room
    temperature
1 cup sugar
½ tablespoon finely grated
    lemon rind
½ cup milk
1 large egg
2 cups all-purpose flour
½ tablespoon baking powder
½ teaspoon salt

1. Preheat oven to 375°F.

2. Combine apple, cinnamon, nutmeg, and lemon juice. Mix thoroughly with a wooden spoon until apple pieces are well coated.

3. In a large mixing bowl, cream butter and sugar with an electric mixer (beat until sugar is dissolved and mixture is creamy). Add lemon rind and milk. Continue to beat until mixture has a light yellow hue and a curdlike consistency resembling ricotta cheese. Add egg and beat until well incorporated.

4. Sift flour, baking powder, and salt together directly into creamed mixture. Blend thoroughly with a wooden spoon. Gently fold in apple pieces, taking care not to dislodge coating.

5. Pour mixture into a greased and floured (bottom and sides dusted with flour) $9\frac{1}{4}$-inch loaf pan. Bake 50 to 55 minutes, until loaf begins to separate from the edges of the pan and a tester inserted into the center comes out clean.

Makes 1 loaf

LEMON RICE BREAD

This distinctive bread almost defies classification. Although it's certainly not savory, it is also not as sweet as one might expect, definitely less so than the popular pudding that inspired its creation.

½ cup (8 tablespoons) unsalted
    butter, melted
1 cup cooked white rice, cooled
    to room temperature
1⅓ cups all-purpose flour
¾ teaspoon baking powder
1½ teaspoons baking soda
¼ teaspoon salt

⅓ cup sugar
1 cup milk
2 large eggs, well beaten
1 teaspoon vanilla extract
½ tablespoon finely grated
    lemon rind
1 teaspoon ground cinnamon
½ cup seedless raisins

1. Preheat oven to 350°F.

2. Mix butter and rice well. Set aside.

3. Sift flour, baking powder, baking soda, salt, and sugar together into a bowl.

4. Combine milk, beaten eggs, and vanilla in a large mixing bowl and whisk together well. Mix in lemon rind, then cinnamon. Add rice mixture and whisk thoroughly. Stir in raisins. Add flour mixture and blend well with a wooden spoon.

5. Pour mixture into a greased and floured (bottom and sides dusted with flour) 9¼-inch loaf pan. Bake 40 to 50 minutes, until loaf begins to separate from the edges of the pan and a tester inserted into the center comes out clean.

Makes 1 loaf

5
"I CAN'T BELIEVE IT'S A QUICK BREAD!"

◆

QUICK OLD-FASHIONED PUMPERNICKEL

Who says you can't make a good pumpernickel without yeast? This is one of our favorite quick breads, with all the richness of flavor and density of texture that characterize the traditional yeast bread.

1¼ cups all-purpose flour
1¼ cups medium rye flour
2 teaspoons baking powder
1 teaspoon baking soda
1 teaspoon salt
1 large egg
1 cup buttermilk

¼ cup dark unsulphured
   molasses
½ tablespoon instant coffee
   granules
2 tablespoons unsalted butter,
   melted
1 cup seedless raisins

1. Preheat oven to 375°F.

2. Sift flours, baking powder, baking soda, and salt together into a bowl.

3. Using an electric mixer, beat egg well in a large mixing bowl. Add buttermilk, molasses, coffee, and melted butter. Beat all ingredients together well.

4. Add flour mixture and raisins. Blend thoroughly with a wooden spoon.

5. Grease a 9¼-inch loaf pan. Cut wax paper to fit the bottom of the loaf pan, grease one side, and place in pan, greased side up. Pour mixture (which will be thick) into pan. Bake 50 to 55 minutes, until loaf begins to separate from the edges of the pan and a tester inserted into the center comes out clean.

Makes 1 loaf

BRAIDED EGG BREAD

We're rather proud of this yeastless wonder. Bearing a bit of a resemblance to a brioche and perhaps related to a challah, it's certainly not a typical quick bread.

BREAD
2½ cups all-purpose flour
2½ teaspoons baking powder
½ teaspoon salt
1 teaspoon sugar
2 large eggs
3 tablespoons unsalted butter, melted
¼ cup warm water
¼ cup milk

TOPPING
1 egg beaten with 1 tablespoon water to paint dough
1 tablespoon sesame seeds

1. Preheat oven to 350°F.

2. Sift flour, baking powder, salt, and sugar together into a bowl.

3. In a large mixing bowl, beat eggs until frothy with an electric mixer. Add melted butter, beating constantly. While continuing to beat, add water and milk.

4. Add flour mixture and stir with a wooden spoon. Continue to mix until a ball of dough is formed. Divide dough into three equal portions. With lightly floured hands, work each portion of dough into a thin strip about 12 inches long and 1 inch in diameter.

5. Lay strips side by side, about ½ inch apart, on a lightly greased cookie sheet that has been dusted with flour. Crimp strips together at the top and braid like a ponytail. Tuck ends under. Paint exposed surface of dough with egg and water mixture, using a pastry brush. Sprinkle sesame seeds on top. Bake 25 to 30 minutes, until a tester inserted into the side of the loaf comes out clean.

Makes 1 loaf

NEW YORK CARAWAY ONION RYE

You can take the boy out of New York, but you can't take New York out of the boy. Barry was determined to come up with a "quick" recipe for a hearty peasant rye—and here it is. Just tear off hunks to serve with stew on a cold winter's night, or serve as the perfect accompaniment to chilled gazpacho in the good old summertime.

BREAD
2 cups all-purpose flour
1⅛ cups stone-ground rye flour
2 teaspoons baking powder
1 teaspoon baking soda
1½ teaspoons salt
2 tablespoons sugar
1 large egg, room temperature
1 cup buttermilk, room
    temperature
2 tablespoons vegetable oil, plus
    1 tablespoon to grease
    baking pan
1½ tablespoons caraway seeds
½ cup finely chopped white
    onion
1 tablespoon white vinegar
½ tablespoon yellow cornmeal

TOPPING
1 egg beaten with 1 tablespoon
    water to paint dough

1. Preheat oven to 375°F.

2. Sift flours, baking powder, baking soda, salt, and sugar together into a bowl.

3. In a large mixing bowl, beat egg well with an electric mixer. While continuing to beat, add buttermilk and vegetable oil, mixing well after each addition. Beat in caraway seeds, then onion, then vinegar.

4. Grease a 9-inch round baking pan with vegetable oil and dust the bottom with cornmeal.

5. Stir flour mixture into the wet ingredients in the large mixing bowl. Dust hands with flour and knead dough lightly for about 30 seconds, working in any excess flour that remains in the bowl. Form dough into a ball and transfer to the baking pan. Press down lightly to spread dough, leaving about a 1-inch border around dough in bottom of pan.

6. Paint egg and water mixture on exposed surface of dough with a pastry brush. Using a very sharp knife that has been dipped in flour, cut a shallow "X" across most of the top. Bake 35 to 45 minutes, until a tester inserted into the center comes out clean.

Makes 1 loaf

ROSEMARY GARLIC BREAD

This is an elegant herbed rendition of garlic bread. But don't worry, it still packs enough of a punch to keep any creatures of the night well at bay.

BREAD
2½ cups all-purpose flour
2½ teaspoons baking powder
½ teaspoon baking soda
½ teaspoon salt
1 teaspoon sugar
2 large eggs
½ cup buttermilk

TOPPING
½ cup (8 tablespoons) unsalted
      butter, melted
1 tablespoon crushed garlic
1½ teaspoons crushed dried
      rosemary leaves

1. Preheat oven to 350°F.

2. Sift flour, baking powder, baking soda, salt, and sugar together into a bowl.

3. In a large mixing bowl, beat eggs until frothy with an electric mixer. While continuing to beat, add buttermilk.

4. Add flour mixture and blend thoroughly with a wooden spoon.

5. Pour mixture into a greased and floured (bottom and sides dusted with flour) 9¼-inch loaf pan. With a sharp knife, make a slight incision most of the way down the middle of the dough. Bake for 20 minutes.

6. Toward the end of this baking cycle, mix melted butter, garlic, and rosemary. Using a well-insulated pot holder, carefully remove loaf pan from oven. Deepen the slit down the middle of the dough (or cut a new slit if the incision has closed). Slowly pour butter mixture into the slit, allowing bread to absorb as much as possible. Paint the top of the loaf with remaining mixture. Bake another 15 to 20 minutes, until loaf begins to separate from the edges of the pan and a tester inserted into the center comes out clean.

Makes 1 loaf

PATTY'S PEPPER CHEESE BREAD

Our friend Patty, who just can't get enough peppery, spicy food, suggested this bread. If, like Patty, you want to go the limit, stir ¼ teaspoon dried red pepper flakes into the mixture after sifting.

BREAD
1 large egg
⅔ cup milk
¼ cup (4 tablespoons) unsalted
    butter, melted
2 cups all-purpose flour
1 tablespoon baking powder
½ teaspoon salt
½ teaspoon sugar
1 tablespoon freshly ground
    black pepper
¼ teaspoon dried red pepper
    flakes, if desired
1 cup shredded provolone
    cheese

TOPPING
1 egg beaten with 1 tablespoon
    water to paint dough

1. Preheat oven to 350°F.

2. In a large mixing bowl, beat egg. Whisk in milk, then melted butter. Sift flour, baking powder, salt, sugar, and black pepper together directly into the mixture. Stir in red pepper flakes, if desired. Mix with a wooden spoon until a ball of dough is formed.

3. Transfer dough onto a 1½- to 2-foot-long sheet of wax paper. Lay a second sheet of wax paper on top of the dough. Using a rolling pin, flatten and shape dough to an oblong about ½ inch thick. Remove the top sheet of wax paper.

4. Lay provolone cheese lengthwise over the bottom third of the flattened dough, leaving a ¼-inch outer border.

5. Raise the wax paper alongside the area where cheese has been spread and roll dough continuously over onto itself to form a log, then crimp the ends.

6. Place seam side down on a greased cookie sheet that has been dusted with flour, tucking ends under. Paint exposed surface of dough with egg and water mixture, using a pastry brush. With a sharp knife, make 2 slight diagonal incisions on top of dough (each about a third of the way along loaf). Bake 25 to 30 minutes, until a tester inserted into the side of the loaf comes out clean.

Makes 1 loaf

PESTO BREAD

For those of us now addicted to the stuff, it's hard to believe that pesto was still a novelty only a few years ago. We love it and just had to make it into a bread. The basil smells incredible, the cheese and oil are rich, the garlic is ever so pungent, and oh, the crunch of the pignoli!

BREAD
½ cup fresh basil leaves, washed
      and dried
1 heaping tablespoon sliced
      garlic
¼ cup grated Parmesan cheese
6 tablespoons olive oil
1 large egg
⅔ cup milk
¼ cup (4 tablespoons) unsalted
      butter, melted
2¼ cups all-purpose flour
1 tablespoon baking powder
½ teaspoon salt
½ teaspoon sugar
2 tablespoons whole pine nuts
½ cup shredded mozzarella
      cheese

TOPPING
1 beaten egg to paint dough
Freshly ground black pepper to
      taste

1. Preheat oven to 350°F.

2. Put basil, garlic, Parmesan cheese, and 1 teaspoon of the olive oil in the bowl of a food processor. While pureeing, drizzle remaining olive oil in through the feed tube. Continue until all of the oil has been absorbed and a paste is formed.

3. In a large mixing bowl, beat egg. Whisk in milk, then melted butter. Sift flour, baking powder, salt, and sugar together directly into the mixture. Mix with a wooden spoon until a ball of dough is formed.

4. Transfer dough to a 1½- to 2-foot-long sheet of wax paper. Lay a second sheet of wax paper on top of the dough. Using a rolling pin, flatten and shape dough to form an oblong about ½ inch thick. Remove the top sheet of wax paper.

5. Spread basil mixture over the flattened dough. Sprinkle pine nuts over the bottom third lengthwise and layer mozzarella cheese on the top two thirds, allowing a ¼-inch outer border.

6. Raise the bottom of the wax paper and fold dough continuously up onto itself to form a log, then crimp the ends.

7. Place seam side down on a greased cookie sheet that has been dusted with flour, tucking ends under. Paint exposed surface of dough with beaten egg, using a pastry brush. With a sharp knife, make 2 slight diagonal incisions on top of dough (each about a third of the way along loaf). Grind fresh pepper on the top. Bake 25 to 30 minutes, until a tester inserted into the side of the loaf comes out clean. Serve hot.

Makes 1 loaf

CHOCOLATE CHIP BABKA

Just like the yeast version after which it is modeled, this babka, or "grandmother's loaf" in Russian, is dense, rich, and sweet.

BREAD
2 cups all-purpose flour, plus
    2 tablespoons to roll dough
    ball in
2¼ teaspoons baking powder
¾ teaspoon baking soda
½ teaspoon salt
3 tablespoons plus 1 teaspoon
    sugar, divided
1 3-ounce package cream
    cheese, softened to room
    temperature
¼ cup milk
2 large eggs, well beaten
¼ cup (4 tablespoons) unsalted
    butter, 2 tablespoons
    melted and 2 tablespoons
    cut into thin pats
¾ cup mini chocolate chips
¼ cup pitted and halved
    maraschino cherries

TOPPING
1 tablespoon milk to paint
    dough
2 tablespoons unsalted butter,
    softened to room
    temperature
¼ cup all-purpose flour
1 teaspoon sugar

1. Preheat oven to 350°F.

2. Sift flour, baking powder, baking soda, salt, and 3 tablespoons of the sugar together into a bowl.

3. In a large mixing bowl, cream the cream cheese and milk (beat until well blended and creamy) with an electric mixer. While continuing to beat, add beaten eggs. Beat in melted butter until mixture is frothy.

4. Add flour mixture and stir with a wooden spoon until a ball of dough is formed.

5. Sprinkle 2 tablespoons flour onto a 1½- to 2-foot-long sheet of wax paper. Transfer dough to wax paper and roll until covered with flour. Lay a second sheet of wax paper on top of the dough. Press down with your hand and spread dough evenly into an oblong about ¼ inch thick. Remove the top sheet of wax paper.

6. Sprinkle mini chocolate chips over flattened dough, leaving about a 1-inch border. Push chips lightly into dough and sprinkle with remaining 1 teaspoon of sugar. Lay pats of butter over surface. Scatter cherries on top.

7. Raise the left-hand side of the wax paper and fold dough continuously over onto itself to form a log, then crimp the ends.

8. Place seam side down in a greased and floured (bottom and sides dusted with flour) 9¼-inch loaf pan, tucking ends under. Paint exposed surface of dough with milk, using a pastry brush. With a sharp knife, make a slight incision most of the way down the middle of the dough.

9. For topping, combine butter, flour, and sugar in a bowl. Blend until crumbly with a large butter knife, cutting up butter to the size of large peas. Sprinkle mixture over loaf. Bake 40 to 50 minutes, until loaf begins to separate from the edges of the pan and a tester inserted into the center comes out clean.

Makes 1 loaf

CREAM CHEESE PINEAPPLE LOAF

There's something rather sinful about a dessert bread that tastes this good but is so ridiculously easy to make. Rich, creamy, and tropical, this filled bread is sure to go fast, so you might want to double the recipe and make two loaves.

BREAD
⅓ cup buttermilk
½ cup sour cream
2 large eggs, well beaten
2¼ cups all-purpose flour (you
    may need to add 1 to 2
    additional tablespoons
    when shaping dough), plus
    2 tablespoons to roll dough
    ball in
2½ teaspoons baking powder
¾ teaspoon baking soda
¼ teaspoon salt
¼ cup sugar

6 ounces cream cheese (2
    3-ounce packages or ¾ of 1
    8-ounce package), softened
    to room temperature
¼ cup milk
1 small can crushed pineapple
    (about 8 ounces), drained
    well

TOPPING
2 tablespoons milk to paint
    dough
¼ cup blanched, slivered
    almonds

1. Preheat oven to 350°F.

2. Put buttermilk and sour cream in a large mixing bowl and beat with an electric mixer. Mix in beaten eggs.

3. Sift flour, baking powder, baking soda, salt, and sugar together directly into mixture.

4. Mix with a wooden spoon until crumbly. With lightly floured hands, form dough into a ball (adding 1 to 2 tablespoons flour if needed).

5. Sprinkle 2 tablespoons flour onto a 1½- to 2-foot-long sheet of wax paper. Transfer dough ball to wax paper and roll until coated with flour. Lay a second sheet of wax paper on top of the dough and press down with your hand to spread dough evenly until about ½ inch thick. Remove the top sheet of wax paper.

6. Whisk cream cheese and milk together until well blended. Whisk in pineapple. Spread mixture lengthwise over the middle third of the flattened dough, leaving a slight border on each side.

7. Raise the bottom of the wax paper and fold dough about halfway up onto itself, taking care not to force the filling out. Fold top of dough down just to overlap, then crimp ends to completely enclose filling.

8. Carefully turn dough over and place seam side down, tucking ends under, on a greased cookie sheet that has been dusted with flour. Brush off any excess flour residue on dough. Paint exposed surface of dough with milk, using a pastry brush. Sprinkle slivered almonds over top. With a sharp knife, make a slight incision most of the way down the middle of the dough. Bake 25 to 30 minutes, until a tester inserted into the side of the loaf comes out clean.

9. When done, let cool slightly on cookie sheet. (Do not attempt to transfer to rack, as loaf could crack.) Serve warm or reheat in a microwave oven set at full power for about 30 seconds.

Makes 1 loaf

INDEX

All-Time Favorite Breads, 6–23. *See also* Favorite Breads
Almond Olive Bread, 26
Apple Cinnamon Swirl, Claudia's, 94
Applesauce Nut Bread, 58
Apricot Cranberry Loaf, 76
Apricot Cream Cheese Swirl, 88

Babka, Chocolate Chip, 108
Banana Bread
    Golden Nut, 17
    Peanut Chocolate, 15
    Traditional, 16

Banned-in-Boston Brown Bread, 40
Beer Bread, Old-Fashioned, 22
Betty Morrissey's Irish Soda Bread, 38
Blueberry Sour Cream Streusel, 18
Blueberry Wild Rice Bread, 19
Bobbi's Raisin Rum Tea Bread, 60
Braided Egg Bread, 99
Brandied Sweet Potato Bread, 44
Bran Honey Bear Bread, 33
Brown Bread, Banned-in-Boston, 40

Bubba's Poppy Seed Bread, 82
Butterscotch–Butterscotch Chip Bread, 81

Caraway Onion Rye, New York, 100
Caraway Tea Bread, 32
Cheddar Cheese Cornbread, 52
Cheddar Dill Bread, 50
Cheese Bread. *See also* Cheddar; Cream Cheese; Feta; Swiss
Patty's Pepper, 104
and Sausage Loaf, Chi-Town, 30
Strawberry Loaf, 66

Cheesecake Chocolate Chip Bread, Linda's, 93
Cherry. *See* Sour Cherry
Chi-Town Sausage and Cheese Loaf, 30
Chocolate
  Banana Peanut Bread, 15
  Bread, Grandma's, 14
  Chip Babka, 108
  Chip Cheesecake Bread, Linda's, 93
Cinnamon Raisin Bread, 90
Classic Spoonbread, 46
Claudia's Apple Cinnamon Swirl, 94
Coconut, Toasted, Date Bread, 12
Cornbread
  with Bacon, Dixie, 51
  Cheddar Cheese, 52
  Farmhouse, 6
  with Jalapeño Peppers, Pueblo, 8
Cornmeal, Classic Spoonbread, 46
Cranberry Apricot Loaf, 76
Cream Cheese
  Apricot Swirl, 88
  and Pineapple Loaf, 110
  and Salmon Bread, 36

Croque Monsieur Loaf, 55
Curry Scallion Bread, Savory, 34

Dark Zucchini Bread, 53
Date Nut Bread, Sara Bluestein's, 10
Date Toasted Coconut Bread, 12
Dill Cheddar Bread, 50
Dixie Cornbread with Bacon, 51
Door County Sour Cherry Bread, 78

Egg Bread, Braided, 99

Farmhouse Cornbread, 6
Favorite Breads, All-Time, 6–23. *See also* Sweet Breads
  Banana Nut, Golden, 17
  Banana Peanut Chocolate, 15
  Banana, Traditional, 16
  Beer, Old-Fashioned, 22
  Blueberry Sour Cream Streusel, 18
  Blueberry Wild Rice, 19
  Chocolate, Grandma's, 14
  Coconut, Toasted, Date, 12

Cornbread, Farmhouse, 6
Cornbread with Jalapeño Peppers, 8
Date Nut, Sara Bluestein's, 10
Gingerbread, Victorian, 20
Orange Gingerbread, 21
Stout Bread à la Lucy, 23
Feta Cheese and Spinach Loaf, 48
Fig Maple Walnut Bread, 63
Fig and Port Wine Bread, 54
Filbert Papaya Bread, 75
Fresh Herb Bread, 47

Garlic Rosemary Bread, 102
Gingerbread, Orange, 21
Gingerbread, Victorian, 20
Golden Banana Nut Bread, 17
Grandma's Chocolate Bread, 14

Herb Bread, Fresh, 47
Honey Bear Bran Bread, 33
Honey and Pear Brandy Bread, Marcia Jo's, 72

"I Can't Believe its a Quick Bread," 98–110
Irish Soda Bread, Betty Morrissey's, 38

Jill's Oatmeal Raisin Bread, 84

Lemon Poppy Seed Tea Bread, 69
Lemon Rice Bread, 96
Linda's Chocolate Chip Cheesecake Bread, 93

Macadamia Nut Raspberry Delight, 86
Mandarin Orange Nut Bread, 64
Mango Pear Bread, 74
Maple Walnut Fig Bread, 63
Maple Yogurt Bread, Nutty, 87
Marcia Jo's Pear Brandy and Honey Bread, 72
Marmalade Bread, Orange, 80

New York Caraway Onion Rye, 100
Nut(ty) Bread. *See also* Name of Nut
    Applesauce, 58
    Golden Banana, 17

Date, Sara Bluestein's, 10
Mandarin Orange, 64
Maple Yogurt Bread, 87
Prune Bread, 91

Oatmeal Raisin Bread, Jill's, 84
Old-Fashioned Beer Bread, 22
Olive Almond Bread, 26
Olive Swiss Cheese Bread, 28
1890s Raisin Spice Bread, 42
Orange
    Gingerbread, 21
    Mandarin, Nut Bread, 64
    Marmalade Bread, 80
    Pecan Tea Bread, 85

Papaya Filbert Bread, 75
Patty's Pepper Cheese Bread, 104
Peanut Banana Chocolate Bread, 15
Peanut Butter Bread, 41
Pear Brandy and Honey Bread, Marcia Jo's, 72
Pear Mango Bread, 74
Pecan. *See also* Nut(ty)
    Orange Tea Bread, 85

Pepper Cheese Bread, Patty's, 104
Pesto Bread, 106
Pineapple and Cream Cheese Loaf, 110
Pineapple Zucchini Bread, 92
Popover Bread, 45
Poppy Seed Bread, Bubba's, 82
Poppy Seed Lemon Tea Bread, 69
Port Wine and Fig Bread, 54
Prune Bread, Nutty, 91
Pueblo Cornbread with Jalapeño Peppers, 8
Pumpernickel, Quick Old-Fashioned, 98
Pumpkin Pie Bread, 77

Quick Old-Fashioned Pumpernickel, 98
Quick tips
    on equipment and techniques, 3–4
    on ingredients, 2–3

Raisin Bread
    Cinnamon, 90
    Oatmeal, Jill's, 84
    Rum Tea, Bobbi's, 60
    Spice, 1890s, 42

Raspberry Cinnamon
    Swirl, 70
Raspberry Macadamia Nut
    Delight, 86
Rhubarb Bread, 62
Rice Lemon Bread, 96
Rosemary Garlic Bread,
    102
Rye, Caraway Onion, New
    York, 100

Salmon and Cream Cheese
    Bread, 36
Sara Bluestein's Date Nut
    Bread, 10
Sausage and Cheese Loaf,
    Chi-Town, 30
Savory Breads, 26–55
  Brandied Sweet Potato,
      44
  Brown,
      Banned-in-Boston,
      40
  Caraway Onion Rye,
      New York, 100
  Caraway Tea, 32
  Cheddar Cheese
      Cornbread, 52
  Cheddar Dill, 50
  Chi-Town Sausage and
      Cheese Loaf, 30
  Cornbread with Bacon,
      Dixie, 51

Croque Monsieur Loaf,
    55
Egg, Braided, 99
Herb, Fresh, 47
Honey Bear Bran, 33
Irish Soda, Betty
    Morrissey's, 38
Olive Almond, 26
Peanut Butter, 41
Pepper Cheese Bread,
    Patty's, 104
Pesto, 106
Popover, 45
Port Wine and Fig, 54
Pumpernickel, Quick
    Old-Fashioned, 98
Raisin Spice, 1890s, 42
Rosemary Garlic Bread,
    102
Salmon and Cream
    Cheese, 36
Scallion Curry, 34
Spinach and Feta
    Cheese Loaf, 48
Spoonbread, Classic, 46
Swiss Cheese Olive, 28
Zucchini, Dark, 53
Savory Scallion Curry
    Bread, 34
Scallion Curry Bread,
    Savory, 34
Soda Bread, Irish, Betty
    Morrissey's, 38

Sour Cherry Bread, Door
    County, 78
Spice Raisin Bread, 42
Spinach and Feta Cheese
    Loaf, 48
Spoonbread, Classic, 46
Stout Bread la Lucy, 23
Strawberry Cheese Loaf,
    66
Strawberry Walnut Bread,
    68
Streusel, Blueberry Sour
    Cream, 18
Sweet Breads, 58–96. See
    also Favorite Breads
  Apple Cinnamon Swirl,
      Claudia's, 94
  Applesauce Nut, 58
  Apricot Cream Cheese
      Swirl, 88
  Butterscotch–Butterscotch
      Chip, 81
  Chocolate Chip Babka, 108
  Chocolate Chip
      Cheesecake, Linda's,
      93
  Cinnamon Raisin, 90
  Cranberry Apricot Loaf,
      76
  Cream Cheese and
      Pineapple Loaf, 110
  Lemon Poppy Seed Tea,
      69

Lemon Rice, 96
Maple Walnut Fig, 63
Nutty Maple Yogurt, 87
Nutty Prune, 91
Oatmeal Raisin, Jill's, 84
Orange, Mandarin, Nut, 64
Orange Marmalade, 80
Orange Pecan Tea, 85
Papaya Filbert, 75
Pear Brandy and Honey, Marcia Jo's, 72
Pear Mango, 74
Pineapple Zucchini, 92
Poppy Seed, Bubba's, 82
Pumpkin Pie, 77
Raisin Rum Tea, Bobbi's, 60
Raspberry Cinnamon Swirl, 70

Raspberry Macadamia Nut Delight, 86
Rhubarb, 62
Sour Cherry, Door County, 78
Strawberry Cheese Loaf, 66
Strawberry Walnut, 68
Sweet Potato Bread, Brandied, 44
Swiss Cheese Olive Bread, 28

Tea Bread
  Caraway, 32
  Lemon Poppy Seed, 69
  Orange Pecan, 85
  Raisin Rum, Bobbi's, 60

Toasted Coconut Date Bread, 12
Traditional Breads. *See also* Favorite Breads
  Banana Bread, 16

Victorian Gingerbread, 20

Walnut. *See also* Nut(ty)
  Strawberry Bread, 68
Wild Rice Blueberry Bread, 19

Yogurt Nutty Maple Bread, 87

Zucchini Bread, Dark, 53
Zucchini Pineapple Bread, 92